ENGLISH RECUSANT LITERATURE
1558–1640

Selected and Edited by
D. M. ROGERS

Volume 158

NICOLAS CAUSSIN

The Christian Diurnal
. . . Reviewed, and
Much Augmented
1640

NICOLAS CAUSSIN

*The Christian Diurnal
. . . Reviewed, and
Much Augmented
1640*

The Scolar Press
1973

ISBN 0 85967 118 6

Published and Printed in Great Britain by
The Scolar Press Limited, 20 Main Street,
Menston, Yorkshire, England

NOTE

Reproduced (original size) from a copy in the library of St. Edmund's College, Ware, by permission of the President.

Reference: Allison and Rogers 216; not in STC.

THE
CHRISTIAN
DIVRNAL.

OF

F. N. CAVSSIN, S. I. re-
viewed, and much
augmented.

And tranſlated into Engliſh,

By Sr T. H.

SECOND EDITION.

By Iohn le Couſturier.

M. DC. XL.

TO
THE RIGHT
HONOVRABLE
THE LADY
Viscontesse Sauage.

*M*ADAME,
*though hea-
uen hath
propitiously*
disposed *your wel-recti-
fyed soule to* Piety *, and
that many* Bookes *of this
kind want not to entertai-*

A 2   *ne*

Epistle.

ne your pious retirements
in the sweete solitude of
Meditation; yet may I
boldly say this Manuall of
deuotion hath some what
new, and attractiue in it,
to add increase of feruor
to your best progression;
and will (I doubt not)
vnder the happy patro-
nage of your Honour (as
from so noble an example)
gaine the serious atten-
tion ; and good opinion of
many, who shall read it,
Congestred Rules , and
multiplicity of precepts,
which onely augment the
                      bulke

bulke of bookes and litle
edify, or informe the mind
are hcere purpoſely auoy-
ded. Short acts of deuo-
tion, and pious aſpirati-
ons more penetrate and
being (as in this Diurnall)
put into methode, winne
vpon the drowzy ſoule;
and open the heart to more
awakned thoughts of ſal-
uation. My ayme in this
Tranſlation, excellent Lady, is your particular contentment, and conſequẽtly
in ſome meaſure to diſ-
charge the obligation I
owe to your much Honou-

A 3   red

red *Family*, the known worth whereof, though it can receaue litle illuftration from the weake indeauours of my pen; yet, should I not at leaft, thus gratefully remember it, hauing fo fayre an opportunity. as this prefent dedication, would make him guilty of ingratitude who with his readieft feruice refolues euer to remaine.

Your honors humbleft feruant,

THOMAS HAVVKINS.

To

TO
MADAME,
MADAME
THE
PRINCESSE.

ADAME,

This Diurnall, since it hath had the honour of your approbation, presumes to appeare vnder your name; and the confidéce it hath taken from

the fauor of your iudg-
ment, makes it hope
your good acceptance.
I had againe publifhed
it, imperfect, without
title, & protection, but
it hauing pleafed your
Excellency to adopt it,
it is augmented, and
embellifhed with time,
refsēbling riuers which
fwel, and purifie them-
felues by their ftreams,
to become tributary to
the fea.

It is an incompara-
ble happineffe for it to
be once more diuulged
vnder

vnder the patronage of
so great a Princesse,
whose extraction hath
nothing in it but subli-
myties, aspect but gra-
ces, heart but generosi-
ties, soule but vertues,
and vertues but admi-
ration. The Altars daily
teach vs the vowes, and
adoratiõs of your High-
nesse, Monasteries of
religious womẽ (which
are your fortunate. I-
lands) preach vnto vs
your piety, the Court,
your excellent perfec-
tions; prosperity, your
mode.

moderation, aduersity.
Your constancy; & all
the world ecchoeth
forth your Goodnesse.
There would not all-
most be any thing like
vnto you, in your sexe,
had you not an onely
daughter , which in
mind and body hath all
the figures of the most
exquisit Maister-pieces
of God.

Giue (Madame) to
heauen all those ritch
endowments, & amidst
the splendors of Court,
where so many liue, as
in

in an enchaūted pallace
(sometimes happy by
illusion , .and alwayes
slaues by necessity)
breath more deliciously
(then euer) the ayre of
your deuotions, to an-
ticipate heauen in your
thoughts. I, for this
purpose present you
with a Diurnall, but the
Creator , and the Fa-
ther of Ages, will giue
you Eternity , which I
ardently wish you, ma-
king profession to ho-
nour you , before God
by my prayers, and be-
fore

fore men by the du-
teous respects , which
I offer you vnder the
title, (MADAME) of

*Your most humble,
and most obedient ser-
uant in our Lord,*

Nicholas Cauffin.

The

THE DESSIGNE OF
the Authour.

I HAVE spoken of the
practise of vertues in the
Booke of the holy Court.
Take heereof in this, some
small scatling for your daily
Actiōs, which ought rather
to entertaine your heart,
then your Eies; It is compendious in reading, but if
you consider it in Action,
you shall in it find in one
Iournall, yeares, and Ages
of Felicity.

The trueth is we haue at
this Time very many spiri-
tual Bookes, which answere
one another like Ecchoes.

This

This Age, is as fruitfull in wordes, as it is barren in good workes, and seemeth willing to speake all, and do nothing; suffering the best part of witt; to vapour out, either by the pen, or tongue. Yet in matter of Piety we may well thinke, one cannot say, that thing, too much, which can neuer be done too much, as allso that in such a penury of worthy acts, we ought not to be sparing of good wordes.

I offer this short Treatise vnto you, to hold it in your hands, as the litle clock, which a great Prince bare in a ring: It striketh all the howers of the day, & corre-
spondeth

fpondeth to Reafon, as true
Dyalls with the Sun.

If you reade it attentiuely
you fhall find it great in its
litlenelfe, ritch in its pouerty, & large in its breuity.

Great Bookes make vs
fometimes more learned,
but not alwayes more innocent : This placeth wifdome
in practife, and happineffe
in piety : You fhall know
what it is, in often reading
it, and in doing what it
fayeth : For it defireth no
other character of its worth
and merit, but, that, of
your vertue.

THE

(❧❧❧❧❧❧❧❧❧❧)

THE DIVISION
of the Diurnal into
fovver partes.

1. *The first part, con-*
taineth Acts of Deuo-
tion.

2. *The second , The*
practise of Vertues.

3. *The third , Af-*
faires.

4. *The fourth, Re-*
creation.

The

THE PRACTISE,
and vse of the Diurnal,
& the Table of Prayers.

THe Treatiſes contained
in this litle worke are
different. There are ſome
which may be daily ſaid, as
certaine Prayers : other
which muſt bee looked on
in the manner of medita-
tion, reading them litle, &
often with reflection on
your Actions.

B   F ⅰg

A Table.

„ Haue likewise some considerations proper for euery day in the Weeke.

After these exeercises it is
good

good to vſe ſpiritual readĩg,
as is ſaid in the Page 67,
whither it be the precepts of
this Booke, the life of Saintes, & namely of ſome Saint,
whoſe memory the Church
that day recordeth.

Add to euerie Day the
Hymnes of the Church,
which you haue in the end
of the Booke. They who
haue more leiſure may alſo
excerciſe the petitiõs, which
the Church maketh euery
hower of the day, as it is ex-
preſſed in the Page 534.

Prayers for the time
of Maſſe.
*My God, diſpoſe me to offer to
thee*, pag. 128

B 2　To

A Table.

You may heere deuoutly
say the offices, distinguished
for euerie day of the weeke,
or the Prayers which are in
the Page 534

In the going forward of
the day, the mind ought to
be busied vpon some de-
uout aspirations, vpon affaires, the practise of vertues, & honest recreations, as
is expressed in the Diurnall.
*An excellent practise for deuout
soules, who are affected to the
office of our Lady.* pag. 97

A

A Table.

Exercise of euery weeke, & Prayer for Confession, and Communion.

B 3　　Con-

A Table.

Excercize of Moneths, & the Yeare.

You must considerately read the Treatises of this litle Booke.

One while the maner how to frame your Actiós, which are Adoration, Thanksgiuing, Obl.tion, Contrition, Petition. See the Page 16 & the
sub-

A Table.

The best way is daily to
reade a litle of it in the manner of meditatiõ, to impresse
it well in your memory, &
to appropriate it to your
state and profession.

A TABLE

of the Sections con-
tained in the fovver
partes of the Chri-
ſtian Diurnal.

A Table.

A Table.

A Table.

II. PART.
Of the practise of vertues.

A Table.

III PART.

Of Affaires.

Sect.

A Table.

IIII PART.

Of Recreation.

Sect.

A Table.

The End

A Pra-

A PROFESSION

of the Catholique Faith, which is the foundation of all Deuotion.

I Belieue, and out of a firme belieffe confeffe all the Articles of Faith, which are contained in the Simbole, declared by the holy Romane Church?

I belieue in God the Father omnipotent, Creator of Heauen, and Earth, & of all things vifible, & inuifible. One onely God in Trinity of perfons, of Father, Sonne, & holy Ghoft, who are but one fame Maiefty.

I belieue a true Lord I E-

SVS

svs-Christ the onely
Sonne of God borne of the
Eternal Father before all
Ages, God of God, begotten, not created or made
confubftantiall with the
Father, being but one fame
Effence, one fame wifdom,
one fame power, by whom
all things are made.

I belieue, that he for the
faluation of mankind defcended from heauen, yet
not leauing heauen fince
he wholy replenifhed it
with his Diuinity , and
that he was incarnate, clothing himfelfe with humane nature , by the vertue
of the holy Ghoft : That
he is borne of the moft
blefied

bleſſed virgin Mary, and is made Man, not ceaſing to be God. He is alſo deliue-red ouer to the puniſhment of the Croſſe vnder Pon-tius Pilat Gouernor of Iury, ſuffering death to giue vs life, & entring into a Sepul-cher, that we may be borne againe. He roſe againe the third day according to the Prophecyes, and aſcending into heauen ſitteth at the right hand of his Father, frō vvhence he ſhall come a-gaine, crowned with glory, to iudge the quick and the dead, and his raigne ſhall be euerlaſting.

I belieue in the holy Ghoſt the third perſon of

C   the

the blessed Trinity who is
also Lord of al things, & li-
fe-giuing origen , who proceeding from the Father &
the Sonne. is equally wor-
shipped with the Father &
the Sonne, and that it is he,
who hath filled the mouths
of Prophets.

I belieue a Catholique,
and Apostolicall Church, I
confesse a Baptisme for remission of sinnes, expecting
a Resurrection of the dead,
and a life to come.

I admit, and receyue. and
most firmely embrace the
Apostolicall and Ecclesia-
sticall Traditions, and other
obseruations , and constitu-
tions of the same Church.
Likewise

Likewise I proteſt to admit the Scripture according to the Senſe, which the holy Church hath held, and ſtill holdeth; ſince it appertayneth to her to iudge of the true ſenſe, and Interpretation of holy Writ which I wil not otherwiſe vnderſtand, then according to the general Conſent of the Fathers.

I confeſſe alſo, that really and properly there are ſeauen Sacraments of the Euangelicall Law, inſtituted by Ieſus Chriſt, and neceſſary for our Saluation, although all of them be not applyed to euery one;

That is to wit, Baptiſme,

C 2　　Con-

Confirmation, the Eucha-
riſt, Pennance, Extreme vn-
ction, Orders, & Mariage.
Al conferre Grace, and
three among them, which
are Orders, Baptiſme, and
Confirmation, cannot be
reiterated without ſacri-
ledge. I embrace the rites
and Ceremonies approued
by the Catholique Church
in the ſolemne adminiſtra-
tion of the ſaid Sacraméts.

I belieue that Originall
ſinne went into the whole
Maſſe of man-kind by the
ſinne of Adam, and cannot
be taken away but by Ba-
ptiſme. And that we are iu-
ſtified by the Infuſion of
Grace, and Charity, which
is

is spred in our hearts by
the merits of the bloud of
Iesus Christ, and by the o-
peration of the holy Ghost.

I likewise hold that in
the Masse, a sacrifice is offered to God, true, proper &
propitiatory for the liuing
and the dead, and that the
body, and Bloud togeather
with the soule, and the Diuinity of our Lord Iesus
Christ is truelie, really, and
substantially in the most
blessed Sacramēt of the Eucharist & that there is made
a chaunge of the whole sub-
stāce of Bread into the Body,
and of the whole substance
of wine into the Bloud of
our Sauiour, which the

C 3   Church

Church calleth by the word Tranfubftantiation. Alfo that vnder cyther of the two kindes Iefus Chrift is, & is receyued wholy without want, or Diuifion.

I firmely hold there is a Purgatory, vvhich is a third place betweene Heauen and Hel, where fome foules being not as yet fufficiently purified to enter into Heauen, are detayned, and are ayded by the praiers of Chriftians.

I likewife auerre the Saints are to he honoured, which raigne with Iefus Chrift, and that they offer vp their praiers for vs to God, and that their very

reliques

reliques, as hauing beene
animated with ſo holy ſoules, are worthy of honour.

I likewiſe cōfidently keep
the Images of Ieſus Chriſt,
and of the bleſſed Mother
of God, euer a Virgin, & in
the like maner of other
Sainƈts to afford them due
reuerence.

I beſides confeſſe that the
power of Indulgencyes was
left vnto the Church by
Ieſus Chriſt, and that the vſe
of them among Chriſtians
is wholeſome.

I acknowledge the Catho-
lique Apoſtolicall, and Ro-
mane Church to be the
Mother and Miſtreſſe of al
Churchs, ſwearing: and pro-
C 4   teſting

A profession
testing true obedience to
the supreme Pope successor
of Saint Peter, who is the
Prince of, Apostles, and the
Vicar of Iesus Christ.

I admit without any
doubt matters graunted, de-
fined, and declared by the
holy Cannons, and the ge-
nerall Counsels, and particularly by the most sacred
Counsell of Trent.

And therefore I condemne
reiect, and detest all things
contrary to this doctrine &
all errors, and Heresyes, ab-
horred, and condemned by
the Church.

I promise, vow, & sweare
to hold, and confesse this
true Faith, by the grace of

God

God, whole, and inuiolable to the laſt breath of my body cauſing it to be preached, and taught to all ſuch as are vnder my charge, and power.

So God helpe, & his holy Euangeliſts.

It is good often to repeate this profeſſion of Faith with Deuotion, and to imprint it well in our memory as the moſt profitable thing which may be learned.

THE

THE
CHRISTIAN
DIVRNAL.

THE FIRST PART.

*The importance of wel ordering
euery Action of the day.*

SECTION I.

A SAGE Father of the Desart cited by Pelagius (an auncient Author) being asked whether the
path

path of Perfection were very long or no, anfwered;All
vertues came togeather,and
that if a man would, he
might in one day arriue to
a kind of Diuinity accor-
ding to his proportion. Verily all our vertues are inclu-
ded in our Actions, and our
Actions in Howers, and the
Howers in the Day, and the
Day in the Moneth, and the
Moneth in the Yeare, and
Yeares in Ages. Euery day
is a compendious Table of
our life; and the meanes to
become quickly perfect, is
to performe all daily actiõs
with great confideration,&
perfectiõ. Behold a draught
heereof, the lineaments of
which

which I haue taken from
many holy Fathers & prime
Authors, adding order, &
embellishment thereto, not
vnprofitable for your direction.

Of the Morning.

SECTION II.

IT is a long time since the
Sun foryour benefit drane
away the shadowes of night
to the end you might de-
light your selfe in the sight
of the great wonders of the
workes of God, and yet are
your Curtaines shut vp to
entertaine you with a dusky
Image

Image of death. Arife from
your bed, &know this goodly Starre, which makes you
begin the carreere of this
day, wil ere night performe
a iourney of a million of
leagues. And (I pray) how
many fteps wil you aduance
in the way of vertue ? This
indefatigable Harbinger is
gone forth, to fcore you out
the lodging of a Tombe; fo
many minutes are fo many
periods deducted from your
life. Will not you follow the
Counfell of the fonne of
God and do good, whilft it
is Day ? A great night wil
very fpeedily involue you
vnder its winges, wherein
you fhal no more haue far-
ther

ther meanes to trauel.

Take euery day as a day in Harueft. Take it as a Faire or Mart. Take it as a day where in you are to labour in the mines of gold. Take it as a ring which you are to engraue, to adorne, & embellifh with your Actiōs, to be offered vp in the Euening at the Altar of God.

Reprefent vnto your felfe a notable confideration of S. Bernard, that your Actiōs paffe without paffing. For euery good worke you doe is a graine of feede for life eternall, Say as Zeuxis that renoumed Painter did, Æternitati pingo. I paint for Eternity.

Follow

Follow the Counsell of S Thomas; do euery Action in the vertue of Iesus Chrift defiring to haue al the good intentions, and affections of the Church militant, and triumphant ; Do it as if thereon depended the honour of God, the good of the whole world your totall happineffe, and as if it were to set a scale vpon all your workes.

Deffigne in the euening the good workes , which you are to performe the next day; what points you are to meditate on, what vice you fhould refift , what vertue excercize, what affaire vndertake, that all may feafonably

nably proceed with a well matured Prouidence. It is the Clew of *Ariadne* which guideth our Actions in the great Labyrinth of Time, otherwise all runneth to Confusion.

Haue sometimes the Curiosity to know of what colour the Day-breake of Morning is, out stripp the steps of light (according to the Counsell of the wiseman) to giue praise vnto God. Take good heed, that you imitate not the Hogge Epicurus, who boasted to haue waxed old, & neuer to haue seene the Sun either rising on setting. It is a good custome to rise in the morning

D ning

ning, but very difficult to
perſuade women ſo, and all
thoſe Antipodes of nature,
who turne day into night, &
night into day. Apollonius
that much celebrated man,
held in his time, for an Oracle of the world, comming
very early in the morning to
Veſpaſian's gate & finding
him awake made a coniec-
ture thereon, that he was
well worthy to command
an Empire, and ſaid to him
that bare him company
Ανηρ ἀρξει, vndoubted by this
man will be Emperor, ſince
he is ſo wakeful.

Al that which you are to
diſpoſe the day vnto, is diuided into fowre partes, 1.
Deuo-

Deuotion, 2. Practise of
vertues, 3. Affaires, and 4.
Recreatiō Deuotion should
cary the Tortch, and open
the gate vnto al our Actiōs.

Make account at your a-
waking, to giue al the firſt
Fruits of your Faculties, of
your Senſes, and your func-
ctiōs to the diuine Maieſty.
Let the memory inſtantly
remember it ſelfe, that it
muſt do the worke of God;
Let the vnderſtanding caſt
a conſideration vpon its
Creator, like a flaſh of
lightnīg; Let the will be enkindled with his loue; Let
the Heart ſhoot forth ſome
fiery ſhaftes, ſome deſires,
and ſome affections wholy
          D 2   cele-

celeſtiall ; Let the mouth &
tongue endeauour to pro-
nounce ſome vocall praiers
to the moſt holy Trinity; Let
the hands lifted vp to heauen make the ſigne of the
Croſſe vpon your forhead
and breſt; Let the armes &
feete ſhake off the ſlugiſh-
neſſe of ſleep as S. Peter did
his chaines at the voice of
the Angel. Behold a good
beginning how to offer ons
ſelfe vp to God. The haire
was pulld off from the victime, and caſt into the fier
before the ſacrifice: So muſt
you take at your awaking
theſe leſſer actions, to giue
beginning to your ſacrifice.

Readily dimiſſe at that
pre-

pretious moment, all the thoughts of affaires, of desires, and of inordinate affections which by heape present themselues and demaund what they are to do. Addresse your selfe to your good Angell, and pray him to offer to God all your actions of the day. Begg of *Iesus Christ* by the most pure conception of his most glorious Mother that all the conceptions, & all the motions of your heart may be for him.

Exercise

D 5.

*Exercise of Deuotion for
the Morning.*

SECTION III.

THE condition of per-
sons is so different and
affaires so diuerse, that it is
very hard to settle any forme
of prayer which may alike
be fit for al. There are some
who partly out of habit,
partly by reason of employment take prayer as it were
running, as the doggs of
Egypt do the water of the
riuer of Nilus. I aduise such
at the least to lift their harts
vp to God when they rise;

to

to adore the most blessed
Trinity, and hauing said the
Pater, the *Aue*, the *Credo*, &
the *Confiteor*, which are the
elements of their beleif, say.

Lord God omnipotent,
who hast preserued mee during the horrors of night,
and hast brought mee to the
beginning of this day, saue
mee by thy vertue, since
thou hast created mee by
thy bountie. Suffer not that
I wander in the darkenesse
of sinne, but graunt that my
thoughts, my wordes, and
my workes, which I harti-
ly offer thee, may this day
be ordered according to the
law of thy diuine will.

Angel of God to whom

D 4   I

I am committed, watch o-
uer my protection and de-
fending mee from all euill,
make mee proceed in good-
nesse, euen to life eternall.

After this they may think
vpon what they are to do,
and suffer that day, propo-
sing to themselues to do &
suffer, all for the glory of
God, and in the midst of
their businesse euer to entertaine some good thought.

As for those who haue
more vnderstanding and lei-
sure, this action should serue
them for a preparatiue to
another deuotion much lō-
ger and more serious, which
they may make in their clo-
set, when they are out of
                    their

their bed. If you haue fo
great a pompe of garments
that you muft beftow fome
notable time to cloath your
felfe, it is a miferable feruitude, do not thinke this is
the way to render your tri-
bute to God, but yet attire
your felf hanfomely as much
as is neceffary both for decency and health. Then
kneele and performe fiue
things, Adoration, Thankf-
giuing, Oblation, Contri-
tion, and Petition.

An Act of Adoration.

You fhall worfhip God,
proftrate on the earth making one in the confort of
the

the great harmony of the
world , offering the whole
vniuerſe to the Creator (as
a votiue Table) hung vp on
his Altar and entirely reſy-
gning your ſelfe to his will.
To this Act aggreeth very
wel the Hymne of the three
Children in the Fournace,
who called al creatures as
by a liſt roule to the praiſes
of God ; or elce take the
forme ; which the Angels
and Saints vſed in adoring
this ſoueraigne Maieſtie,
thus, Holy,holy,holy,Lord
God of Hoaſts , who haſt
bin , who art , and ſhal be.
Thou art worthy , O Lord
our God , to receiue as atri-
bute all glory,all honour,al
vertue:

vertue : For thou art the Creator , and absolute Master of al things. It is thou who hast created both heauen and earth with al their embellishments , thou who boundest the sea by thine Omnipotent word : thou who signest the Abysses with the Seale of thy name; terrible , and praise-worthy for euer : thou who makest the pillars of heauen to treble vnder thy feete : thou, who strikest terror into all creatures by the insupportable lustre of thy Maiestie; Thou who sittest in the Pauilion of thy glory vpon the winges of Cherubins, and from thence dost measure
the

the depth of the Abysse. I
adore thee my God, from
the Center of my nothing,
with all the creatures of the
world, making into thy
hāds a full resignation of all
that, which I am; and desiring to depend for the present, & for all eternitie vpon
thy holy Will.

A Forme of Thanks-giuing.

You shall giue thanks for
all benefits in generall, and
particularly for those which
you receiue at this present,
and which then represent
themselues vnto you, that
you may. season this action
with some nevv tast. The
Church

Church furnisheth vs with an excellent forme of giuing thanks to God in the Hymne, *Te Deum*, or elce say with those most blessed soules.

To thee my God benediction and light, wisdome, and thankf-giuing, honour strength, and vertue in the reuolution of all ages.

My God, O that the glory thou deseruest might be rendred thee at the throne of thy Maiestie and that thy holy peace on earth may be giuen to men of good will. My God I praise the, I blesse the, and I adore thee; I yeild thee thanks for the greatnesse of thy glory and benefits

fits. Great God, King of heauen & earth, eternal Father,
and abfolute Mafter of all
things : And thou alfo Iefus
my Sauiour only fonne of
the heauenly Father , true
God, true Man, who blotteft
out the finners of the world
and fitteft, at the right hand
of the liuing God : And
thou holy Ghoft confub-
ftantial to the Father and to
the Sonne, moft bleffed Tri-
nitie , accept my praier in
thanks-giuing.

*The manner how to offer ones
felfe vp to God.*

O my fweet Sauiour illu-
minate my intentions with
thy

thy lights and support my
weakenesses by thy mercies.
I now recommend vnto thee
the litle seruice, which I do
to the ineffable swetnesse of
thy heart, and hence forth
I sett it before thy eyes to
direct, correct; and perfect
it; I offer it vnto thee with
all I am, with the whole
power of my affectiõs, both
for my selfe, and for al the
faithful, and I offer it vnto
thee in the vnion of that
most exact attention thou
then hadst, when on earth
thou prayedst to thy hea-
uenly Father.

An Act of Contrition.

O Father, I haue sinned
against

against Heauen and before thee vnworthy that I am to carry the name of a sonne, hauing requitted of great goodnesse with contempt, and such benefits with Ingratitude. I complayne not of the punishments which my sinnes haue caused, but I bewayle a God offended, who deserued to be beloued & honoured aboue al thĩgs. Where shall I find punishments enow to auenge me of my selfe, and teares sufficiēt to wash away my sinns? O Father, the face of sinne shall heereafter be more hideous to me then Hell, make me as one of thy Hirelings. O God thou art our

Father

Father, and we are naught
but Earth, and dust in comparison of thee! Thou art
our workman, and wee all
are but clay in thy hands:
My God! be not angry with
an obiect so feeble, so wretched: My God, keepe not
in remembrance the sinnes
of my forepassed life. I purpose by thy grace, speedily
to confesse them, with a full
resolution neuer to returne
to them againe, to vndergo
the pennance which shalbe
imposed me, and to with-
draw my self from occasios,
which haue caused my fall.
I offer vnto thee for satisfa-
ctio the most pretious bloud
of thy sonne, shedd for me

E   out

out of infinite loue , and
with excessiue dolours; hūbly beseeching thee to acept it, and to preserue me,
in the accidents, which may
befall me in my frailty
which is so ordinary, and
frequent.

A Forme of Petition.

My God, giue me , and to
al those whom I recōmend
vnto thee in my prayers an
vnderstanding which may
know thee , an affectionate
deuotion which may seeke
thee , a conuersation which
may please thee , a perseuerance which may couragi-
ously waite on thee, a confidence

dence which may louingly
embrace thee:my God han-
dle the matter so,that I may
be wounded with thy sufferings in my pennance, that
I may in this life vse thy
benifits in grace , and in the
other enioy thy eternall cōforts in the bosome of Glory, Amen.

*As it is good to entertaine
your deuotions with some variety and in so much as the self
same Formes reiterated may be
troublesome I wil heere sett
down the manner so to conceiue
them , that they may sometimes
be said, and not daily repeated.*

A.

*A method how to dispose
Adoration.*

SECTION IV.

YOu are to note that there is a difference be-tweene Praise , Honor, Prudence , and Adoration. Praise properly consisteth in wordes, Honour in exterior signes, Reuerence in interior Respect but Adoration considered in its extent comprehendeth all those Acts with much more eminency. For Adoration is an Act of Religion , whereby we do homage to the soueraignity

ueraignity of God with a
low submission, which is
not in the same degree com-
municable to any creature.

This Act is made, & com-
posed of fowre thigs, which
be (as it were) its fowre elements. The first is a strong
conceit of the greatnesse,
and excellency of God. The
second a consideration of
our basenesse compared to
this supreme Maiesty. The
third a flaming Act of the
wil, which vpō this thought
is wholy dissolued into reuerence; And the fowerth,
an exterior expression both
by the lipps, and gesture of
body; which witnesse the
motions of our heart.

E 2   The

The foule then to performe this Act of Adoration, first of all conceiueth God, great, awfull, replenished with Maiefty, It conceiueth him as a Sea infinit in effence, Goodneffe, and Beatitude, who within himfelfe includeth all Effence, all good, all trueth, and not onely includeth it but from all eternity anticipateth it with an incomparable eminency : It vieweth the whole vniuerfe in the Immenfity of God, as a Spöge would be in the midft of the Ocean, an Atome in the Ayre, and a petty diamond enchafed in the higheft heauen: It knoweth God as the

foun-

foundation of all possible
things the super-essetiall essence, of al things, which are
and are not, without which
nothing subsisteth eyther
in Act, or Power, and hath
no apparance by vvhich the
vnderstāding may lay hold
of it , to haue knowledge
thereof. It figureth God to
it selfe , as the Beginning,
& Ending of all things, the
Creator , Fownder , Basis,
Support, Place, Cōtinuance
Terme, Order, Band, Con-
cord, and Consummation
of al creatures , which containeth within it-selfe al the
good of Angels, of Men, &
of vniuersall nature. Which
hath all glory, all dignities,

all ritches, all treasures, all
pleasures, all consolations,
all delights, all ioyes, & all
Beatitudes, as *Lessius* very
well explicateth in his Treatise of Infinity.

This soule not content
leisurely expatiateth among
the fowerteene Abysses of
Greatnesse which are in God
to wit, Infinity, Immensity
Immutability Eternity, Omnipotency, Wisdome, Perfection, Sanctity, Benignity, Dominion, Prouidence, Mercy. Iustice, and
the end to which all things
tend.

It first considereth euery
perfection absolutely, then
by comparison and application,

tion, making reflection vpõ
it selfe, and comparing this
Infinity of God to its Nothing, this Immensity to its
litlenesse, this Immutabilitie
to its inconstancy. This Eternity to the shortnesse of this
temporall life, this Omnipotency to its Weaknesse, this
Wisdome to its Ignorance,
this Perfection to its Defects, this Sanctity to its vices, this Benignity to its ingratitude, this Dominion to
its pouerty, this Prouidence
to its stupidity, this Mercy
to its obduratenesse, this Iustice to its Iniquity, this End
where vnto all things tend,
to the great dependencyes,
which arise from its Infir-
mityes.   There

There it remaineth wholy
abſorpt in God, as a litle Ant
would be in the Sun, and as
Ariſtotle, who, as it is ſaid,
being vnable to vnderſtand
the floud, and ebb of the Sea
threw himſelfe into it; So it
engulpheth it ſelfe in ſo
many wonders, not meaſu-
ring any more its loue by
the ell of its knowledge.

It ſwooneth in this great
Labyrinth of miracles, much
otherwiſe then the Queene
of Saba did in Salomons
Pallace, and needs muſt it in
the end breake into an Exterior Act, and ſay. *My God
and my all, God of my heart, my
portion.and Enheritance for euer
and euer.*

How

*How Thanks-giuing should be
made, which is the second
Act of Deuotion.*

SECTION V.

THis is an Act very ne-
cessary, considering the
benefits, vvhich vve continually receyue from the
hand of God. It is not fit
vve be like clovvdes vvhich
couer the sun after it hath
rayfed them, but that vve
rather be like a looking
glasse, vvhich rendereth the
Image fo foone as the face
is prefented.

We ought not to let any
benefit

benefit paſſe , comming to
vs from this ſoueraigne
hand, of vvhich vve repre-
ſent not the liuely Image in
our gratefull remembrāces.
And if thoſe auncient He-
brevvs (as vvitneſſeth *Ioſe-*
phus) ſet markes, and ſtain-
pes, ſometimes on their armes, other vvhile on their
Gates, to declare to all the
vvorld the benefits vvhich
God had conferred on their
families , is it not a matter
very requiſite that vve in
ſome ſort endeuour to ac-
knovvledge the liberalities
of the diuine Maieſty.

This Act conſiſteth in
three things: Firſt in the memory, vvhich preſenteth the
bene-

benefits receyued, to the
vnderstanding and the vn-
derstanding considereth the
hand which giueth them,
and to vvhom, and hovv, &
wherefore by vvhat meanes
& in vvhat proportion: Thē
there is framed in the will
an affectionate ackovvledg-
ment, which loth to be idle,
dilateth it selfe in exterior
Acts, to vvitnesse the feruour of its affections.

To practise it throughly,
you must make to your selfe
a list of the benefits of God,
vvhich are cōtained in three
sorts of goodnesse, & mercy.

The first is that, by vvhich
he hath dravvne this great
vniuerse from Abysses, and
the

the darknesse of Nothing to
the light of Essence, & Life,
creating for our sakes a
vvorld vvith so much greatnesse, beauty, vtility, proportion, order, vicissitude,
continuance, and preseruing
it, as it vvere vvith the perpetuall breath of his Spirit,
by affording to euery thing
its raks, forme, proprieties,
appetites, inclination, si-
tuation, limits, and accom-
plishment : But aboue all
creating Man, as a like miracle of Nature, vvith the
adornement of so many pie-
ces, so vvell enchassed, to
beare on the brovv thereof
the rayes of his Maiesty.

The second benignity is,
that,

that, whereby he hath plea-
sed to rayse total nature in
Man to a supernaturall condition : and the third, by
vvhich he hath exalted Humane nature fallen into
Sinne, miseries, and the
shades of death, vnto In-
nocency, Felicity, light, and
eternall life.

The incomprehensible
mistery of the Incarnation
of the Word comprehen-
deth six other benefits, to
vvit, the Guift of the doctrine, & Wisedome of Hea-
uen cõferred on vs; the light
of the good Exãples of our
Sauiour, the Oeconomy of
Redemption, the fauor of
Adoption into the number
                            of

of the children of god; the treasure of the merits of Iesus Christ, and the Banquet of the holy Eucharist; Besides these benefits, vvhich are in the generallity of Christian soules, vve should often represent vvith great humility, the particular fauors receiueth from God, in our Birth Breeding, Education, instruction, Talents, of mind and body, Abilityes, Frends, Alliance, Kinred, vocation, state, profession, continuall preseruation, and deliuerance from so many perils, in the vicissitude of aduersities, & prosperities, & lastly in the order of the degrees of euery Age, wherein

each

each one may in his particular acknowledge many blessings of the diuine Prouidence.

All which remembred by a soule with confideration of the circumstances of euery benefit, euicteth in the end from the will, this act of gratitude, which causeth it to fay that, which the Prophet Dauid fpake : *My God, who am i, and what is the houfe of my Father, that you haue done all this for me?*

E

Ŝ me

*A Method of the Offertory, or
Oblation, which is the third
Act of Denotion.*

SECTION VI.

REligion, and Sacrifice
began from the Birth
of the world, & haue euer
been inseparably tyed to-
gether. God who giueth all,
will that we giue to him, &
is content we take out of
his Treasures, what we cannot find in our nothing.
Novv , obserue a considerable thing, that as in the law
of Moyses, there were three
sortes of Sacrifice , to vvit,
                    Immo-

Immolations, Libations, &
Victimes. Immolations,
vvhich vvere made of the
fruits of the Earth. Libations of liquors, as of Oyle,
and Wine; Victimes of Beastes: So God vvould that for
fruits you giue him your
actions, and for liquours
your affections, and your
selfe for victime. This is
done by the Act of Obla-
tion, or Offertory, vvhich is
a manner of Sacrifice, wherein vve at the aultar of the
diuine Maiesty offer our-
selues, and all that belongeth to vs.

That, we may well per-
forme this Action, first vve
must haue a chast considera-
F 2   tion

tion of the povver and Empire God hath ouer vs. Secondly an intimate knovvledge of the dependence we haue of him, reprefenting to our-felues not onely that vve haue receiued Beeing, and all vvhich waiteth thereon, from his Bounty ; but that vve are ftill each moment fupported by his hand as vvould a ftone be in the aire, and that fhould he flacken euer fo litle , we fhould diffolue into the nothing , from vvhence vve vvere deriued. Thence an Act of Iuftice will arife, in a promptneffe of our will, to render vnto God vvhat appertaineth to him. And as
here-

heretofore the Holocaust was the most noble of Sacrifices, vvhere the Hoast vvas totaly consumed in the honour of the Diuine Maiesty, so we shall imitate this excellent Act, of Religion by consecrating to god, not onely our actions, and affections, but all vve are, desiring to be povvred out, and annihilated for him, if it might be for the honour of his diuine Maiesty.

Novv if this annihilation cannot be reall, vve must at least make it in spirit in some singular manner procuring in ourselues (as much as possible vve can) tvvelue sortes of disengagements, in

vvhich

which the perfection of the Holocauſt conſiſteth.

The firſt, is a diſcharge from all affection of temporall things, ſo that we no lōger loue any thing, but for God, & of God, & according to God. Thé ſecōd is a diſentanglement from proper intereſt in all our actions. The third, an entire mortification from Senſuallity. The fowrth a ſeperation from amityes, ſenſuall, naturall, and acquired, not ſuffering them any longer to lay hold on our heart, to the preiudice of vertue. The fifth, a baniſhment of wordly imaginations, in ſuch manner, that their onely repreſenta-

sentation may in vs breed
an auersion, and horror.
The sixth, an infraunchis-
ment from worldly cares,
not necessary to saluation.
The seauenth, a freedome
from bitternes, and anxieties of heart, which ordinarily spring from ouer
much loue, borne to crea-
tures. The eight, a cou-
ragious flight from all
fortes of vanities of the
mind. The ninth, a con-
tempt of fensible consolations, at such time as God
would haue vs to be wea-
ned from them. The tenth,
an abnegation of scruples of
heart, and proper fanta-
fies, to follow the aduise &
F 4   com-

command of thofe who go-
uerne vs. The eleauenth, a
mitigation of the difturban-
ces which happen in aduer-
fities. The twelfth, an abfolute mortification of iudgement, & will:So that we follow al theinfpiratiõs of God
as true Dyalls do the Sun.

He, who hath therein pro-
ceeded fo farre, maketh a
true annihilation of himfelf,
and an excellent oblation of
all that he is : But if you cannot wholy giue the Tree
with fo much perfeccion, at
leaft yeild the fruits, defiring
laftly to offer vp all your faculties, your fenfes, functiõs,
wordes, workes, and all you
are, remembring the faying
of

of Saint Iohn Chrisostome.
That it is the most wicked aua-
rice that may be to defraud God
of the oblation of ones selfe Offer your memory to the Father to replenish it as a vessel
of Election with things profitable, your vnderstanding
to the Sonne to enlighten it
with eternall verities, your
will to the holy Ghost to enkindle it, with holy ardour;
Consigne your Body to the
blessed Virgin, to gard it vnder the seale of Purity.

The manner of Contrition, the fowrth Act of Denotion.

SECTION VII.

IT is an Act very necessary in such, and so perilous accidents, & so great frailty as ordinarily we do liue in. The learned Theodoret in his questions vpon the Scripture sayth, there are three kindes of life, signified by three sortes of creatures , whereof mention is made in the sacrifice of Abraham in the 15 th. chapter of Genesis. There is 1. a life Animall, represented

fented by fower-footed bea-
ftes; 2. A life mourning fi-
gured in the Turtle; 3. A
life white and pure, whereof the doue is the Hiero-
gliphe. Animall liues are
moft frequent in the world;
Doue-like liues are very rare;
but there is no Doue fo pure
which hath not euer fome
need of the mournig of the
Turtle. And it is for this
caufe why we ouhgt not allmoft at any time to pray,
without ftirring vp fome
acts of Cótrition. Euery one
knowes Contrition is a de-
teftation of finne beyond all
things the moft deteftable,
which takes its Source from
the loue of God, and from
the

the hope of his mercy, and
ought euer to be accompa-
nyed with a firme purpose
of amendment. The firſt foū-
dation is the belieffe of a liuing God, of a God cleare-
ſighted, of a God dreadfull
in all his iudgments, whereby is procured a feare awed
with the paines due vnto
ſinne in hearts the moſt ſtu-
pid. This is the thūder ſtroke
which cauſeth does to fawn,
and raiſeth Tempeſts, and
Earth-quakes in the ſoule.
Then Hope reareth it-ſelfe
aboue the Horiſon, diſper-
ſing amorous rayes out of a
certaine confidence we
haue to obtayne pardon
of our ſinnes, by ſubmit-
ting

ting our felues to the yoke
of Penance. Afterward the
loue of God beginneth in
the foule to free and difcharge it felfe from the In-
terefts of Earth, to produce
in the end this heauenly do-
lour, which is created as pe-
arles from the dew of heauen. Oh a thoufand times
happy thofe, who wafh
themfelues with the waters
of fnow, whereof holy Iob
fpeaketh & purify themfelues in the wholefome Poole
of Penitence.

Stirre vp oftentimes Acts
of Contrition for all finnes
in generall, and particularly
for fome defects and imperfections which moft fur-
charge

charge you with a firme
purpose to resift them manfully, and vtterly to extirpe
them by the helpe of God.

*The manner how to make Pe-
tition. The fift Act of
Deuotion.*

SECTION VIII.

A Great Emperour com-
ming into Egipt, to
witnesse the zeale he bare to
the publique good said to
the Egiptians : Draw from
mee , as from your riuer
Nilus : but what can we
draw

draw from man, but Hopes
which crack as bubles on
the water, so soone as they
are rayfed. It is from God
we muft draw, fince he is
a fountaine, which perpe-
tually runneth, and who
quenching the thirft of all
the world, hath himfelfe
but one which is (as faith
fainct Gregory Nazianzen)
that all mortalls fhould
thirft his Goodneffe.

We muft neceffarily begg
of God, fince our neceffityes
enforce vs thereunto, & his
Bounty inuiteth vs; we muft
aske what himfelfe hath
appointed vs in our Lords
Prayer, which is the Som-
mary

mary of all Theology : we
muſt aske it in the name
of the ſonne, and with confidence to obtaine it we
muſt ,pray for the Church,
for the Paſtors, for our moſt
gratious King, for publi-
que neceſſityes, for our ſelues, and for our neighbours:
we may aske for ſpirituall,
and temporall bleſſings, as
much as ſhall be lawfull for
the good of the ſoule, and
for eternall ſaluation. For
which purpoſe it is good to
haue a collection of prayers
for all' occaſions, as a litle
Fortreſſe furnished with all
mãner of peices of battery,
to force with a religious
aſſault, & a pious violence.

At

At the least daily pray e-
uery morning, that thou offend not God mortally, nor
be wanting in Grace, Light,
and courage to resist those
sinnes to which thou art
most inclined. To practise
the vertues most necessary
for thee. To be guided, and
directed this very day by the
prouidence of God, in all
which concerneth the weale
of soule of body, and exterior things. To participate
in all good workes done
throughout Christendome.
To obtaine new Graces, &
assistances for the necessityes of our neighbours,
which thou mayst then re-
present.

G *Pursuing*

Pursuing this course thou shalt learne to frame these fiue Acts in the manner of mentall praier, according to the thoughts which God shall suggest, or thou shalt take the examples and Formes which I haue brought thereon and thence thou shalt passe to the innocation of the blessed Virgin, and the Saintes.

*Of the Interceßion of Saints, of
which we make vſe in the
Petitions we offer
to God.*

SECTION IX.

AS for the Interceſſion of
Saintes it is good to re-
commend your ſelfe very
particularly to the mother
of God by this auncient
forme.

O my moſt holy miſtreſſe,
I put my ſelfe to day, and
ſo all the daies of my life
into your protection, and
(as it were) into the boſome of your mercyes, I
recommend vnto you my

G 2   ſoule

soule, my body, all that belongeth to me, all my hopes all my affaires, all my difficulties, my miseries, my consolations, and aboue all the manner of my death, to the end, that by your merits, and prayers, all my actions may be directed, according to the Holy will of your sonne.

O most mild Virgin succour the miserable, help the weake, comfort the afflicted, pray for the people, be the Aduocate of persons ecclesiastique, and protectrix of the deuout Sexe. Graunt that all those who celebrate your memory, may this day tast your fauours: but most especially

especially obtaine for me of
your sonne a profound hu-
mility a most vnspotted
chastity, progression, and
perseuerance in goodnesse,
and afford me some small
participation in the dolours
you suffered on the day of
his passion, adding thereunto also some small sparke
of that great deuotion you
did excercise in the holy
Communion after the As-
cention of the Word Incarnate.

*For your Angell Guardian,
saying.*

O God omnipotent, and
eternall, who hast created
me

me to thy Image, and de-
puted one of thy Angells
to defend me, although I
am most vnworthy of this
fauour : Giue me grace I
may now this day escape
all perils of soule , and
body vnder his direction,
and safegard , and graunt
that I in the end after the
course of this life may par-
take in heauen of his glory, whom I on earth haue
for protector.

And.

And to all the Angells by ma-
king prayer in imitation
of the Church.

O God, who with admi-
rable order gouerneſt the
miniſtery of Angells, and
men, ſo do by thy mercy,
that thoſe who are pre-
ſent, and perpetually in
Heauen attend before the
throne of thy Maieſty, may
likewiſe on earth be Gui-
des, and Directors of our
life.

And for all Saints.

Protect thy poore people
(O Lord) and as they haue
a ſingular confidence in the
G 4 pro-

protectiō of thy great Apoſtles S. Peter, and S. Paule,
& of al the reſt of thy Apoſtles, and of all Saintes of
both Sexes, who now liue
in Heauen, preſerue them by
thy gratious aſſiſtance, and
for euer defend them.

---

*Then in memory of thoſe, whoſe
Feſtiualls the Church at this
preſent celebrateth, and
whoſe names are cou-
ched in the Mar-
tyrologe.*

LEt all thy Saints (O
God) who are honou-
red through all the partes of
the world aſſiſt vs, that we
recor-

recording the memory of
their merits, may be sensible of the fauour of their
protection, Giue peace to
our dayes by their interces-
sion, and for euer banish all
malignity from thy Church.
Direct our way, our ac-
tions, our wills in a com-
fortable prosperity, affording Beatitude to our benefactors for the reward of
their charity, and to the
soules of the faithfull departed, euerlasting Rest,
vvhich I most humbly begg
of thee through thy well beloued Sonne.

*They who haue charges and
familyes may say the ensuing
Prayer.*

A

A deuout Prayer drawne out of an auncient Miſſall, to recommend diuers perſons, and neceſsityes.

INeffable Creator, and Soueraigne Lord of all things, I beſeech thee by the ſweetneſſe of thy mercyes, to purify my heart, and lippes, and to make me able to pray vnto thee for all perſons, and neceſſityes which thou wouldſt to be recommended to thee. I, for this cauſe offer vnto thee my moſt humble prayers, for the Supreme Biſhop of the Church, for our moſt Chriſtian King, for our Paſtor, for all thoſe who haue charge

of

of our soules, for the Go-
uernours & Magistrates, and
the whole congregation of
the Faithfull, that it may
please thee to continue vs
all in true Faith, and Religion, & graunt vs the comfort of peace. I particularly
implore thy assistance for
my domestiques, Kinred,
allyes, and Frends, beseeching thee to pardon them the
sinnes they haue committed
to preserue them from daungers, and occasions, which
may cause them to offend
thee, and deliuer them from
enemyes, both visible and inuisible.

Graunt vs (O mercifull
Father) calmnesse ouer
passions

passions, Health of Body,
happy dayes, moderate seasons, and povvre thy bleffings vpon the fruits of the
earth for the sustentation of
the liuing.

Giue likevvise to thy enemyes and vnto vs true charity, comfort in maladies,
returne to pilgrimes, and
trauellers, liberty to prisoners, harbour to sea-fa-
rers, consolation to the afflicted, conuersion to sinners, perseuerance to such as
serue thee, and euerlasting
rest to the deceased.

This I beseech thee by the
most pretious bloud of thy
dearely beloued sonne our
Lord & Sauiour *Iesus Christ*,
by

by the merits of his moſt
bleſſed Mother , and the
Interceſſion of all Saints ,
vvho liue and raigne vvith
thee. So be it.

⚜⚜⚜⚜⚜⚜⚜⚜⚜⚜⚜⚜

Of Meditation and Time fit for
ſpirituall Leſſon, For ſuch
as haue ſome practiſe
therein.

SECTION X.

Theſe fiue Acts well vn-
derſtood vvill be fiue
ſources of meditation , and
other prayers : For if you
vvell obſerue all the eleuations

tions, which are in the Prophet Dauid, and so many other holy vvorkes you shall find they are applyed to these fiue fore-mentioned Heads.

Let me tell you of a notable saying of S. Iohn Climachus, that meditation, (vvhich is prayer of heart) is an infinite operation, & the Horison of the vvorld visible and inuisible; An infinite operation, since it is employed in the perfections of a God infinite, and the Horison, or seperation of the vvorld visible, and inuisible, in so much as it seperateth vs from the condition of vulgar soules, to

giue

giue vs entrance into the
conuerſation of Angels.

And well did S. Bernard
ſay in the fift Book of Conſideration, that Contemplation was an egreſſe from the
Countrey of Body, to go into the Region of Spirits.
Endeuor to diſpoſe your
ſelfe a litle, according to
your capacity to ſo noble an
excerciſe, and diſpaire not
of your ability, if you haue
a good will to vnite your
ſelfe to your Creator.

Do you imagine you ſtand
in need of much eloquence,
& a huge pōpe of prepara-
tion to ſpeake before God?
Belieue me, a heart woun-
ded with loue, is eloquent
enough

enough in the simplicity of
its affections.

The glorious mother S.
Teresa well obferued, that
there were two fortes of
prayer, one mentall, and
the other fupernaturall:
The firft is a riuer, which taketh a long voyage through
a miry Countrey: but the
other is like a chriftaline
fource, which hath no com-
mixtion with the dreggs of
Earth. In the one we go to
God by many obftacles,
which fometimes delay vs,
and many times ftay vs. In
the other, God in a moment
placeth vs neare to himfelfe,
and takes away from vs the
curtaine, to fatiate vs with
the

the fight of his verities. All
that, which is infpired is in-
comparably more forcible,
then what is ftudyed. How
many fimple foules thinke
you are there; who haue a
great facility to treate with
God, and albeit they are
ignorant in the iudgment of
the world, are knowing before him.

If you haue not the guift, of
prayer, begg it inceffantly of
God, employing a good life
to be your aduocate. You
may learne from your Director, and out of fo many
good bookes the manner
how to prepare your felfe
thereto ; You know what
the fortes of meditation

H   are

are, which you shall in the morning orderly difpofe, one while vpon the benefits of God, another while on his greatneffe, fometimes ou the fower laft ends, fometimes on the Symbole, and the Commandments, fometimes on vices & vertues, and vpon all the inftructions contained in this prefent Booke, but aboue all vpon the life and death of our Sauiour.

You are not ignorát how that after you haue placed your felfe in the prefence of the liuing God, after you haue inuoqued the light of his holy Spirit, after you ha e conceiued the fubiect

of

of your meditation, you
muſt ſtay in thought therevpon, to draw from thence
conſiderations, affections,
inſtructions, and ſuteable
reſolutions. If you can do
nothing els, attetiuely reade
ſome good Booke take
thoſe words of the doctrine
of our Sauiour, which I
haue heere beneath inſerted, make a litle pauſe vpon euery article, pondering on the verity of that
Sentence, and how you
haue obſerued it, and
what you will do hereafter to put in practiſe. All
which is in this litle
booke (were it well confide-

red)would furnith you with matter, profitably to entertaine your thoughts, and feed you foule with the nutriment of verity.

If you will belieue me, at this very fame inftant of the morning, when your mind is moft difengaged from terreftrial thoughts , you should practife fpirituall leffons reading fometimes holefome precepts, otherwhile the liues of Saintes, remembring what S. Ifodore fayd in his booke of Sentences. That he who will liue in the exercife of the prefence of God, muft often pray, and read; when you pray you fpeake to

God,

God, & when you read God
fpeaketh to you : Good Ser-
mons, and good Bookes are
the finewes of vertue.

Do you not confider, that
colours, as Philofophy teacheth, haue a certaine light,
which in the night time is
dulled, and as it were buried
in matter: But fo foone as
the fun rifeth, and openeth
his rayes ouer fo many bewtyes languifhing in dark-
neffe, he awakeneth them,
and makes them appeare in
their proper luftre. So we
may truely fay, that we all
haue certaine feedes of wifdome, which amidft the va-
pours caufed by our paf-
fion remaine as it were
H 3   wholy

wholy choked, if the wifdome of God, which fpeaketh in holy Scriptures, and good fpirituall Bookes did not rayfe them, affording them fplendor, and vigor, to enkindle the race of our actiõs to vertue. Perpetually inuoke the Father of light, before you take your booke in hand, to direct your reading: Read litle if you haue litle leifure, but with attétion; & often ftay vpon fome fentence, which you may often in the courfe of the day call to memory: you fhall find, that what good Bookes teach is wholy Trueth, what they cõmand is goodneffe, & what they promife, Felicity.

Deue-

Deuotion according to the order
of the daies of the weeke,
to fit some small conside-
ration to euery day.

SECTION XI.

IF you desire this diuision
of daies, I must tell you,
that some dedicate Sunday,
to the most blessed Trinity;
Monday, to the comfort of
faithfull soules which are
departed into the other
world; Tuesday, to the memory of Angels, Wednes-
day, to that of the Apostles, and of all Saintes;
Thurs-

Thursday to the veneration
of the Sacrament of the Altar; Friday, to the miftery of
the Paffion; and Saturday
to the honour of our Lady.

Other employ their me-
mory to be particular for
euery day, as for Sunday,
the glory of Heauen; Mon-
day, the day of Iudgment;
Tuefday, the bleffings of
God; Wednefday, death;
Thurfday, the paines of hel;
Friday, the Paffion; Saturday, the vertues of our Lady,
as before: This is the counfell of S. Bonauenture in his
leffer workes.

We alfo deriue a fingu-
lar practife of deuotion for
euery day of Weeke from
                        the

the Hymnes of Saint Ambrose, vvhich the Church perpetually makes vfe of. For from thence we learne to giue God thankes, for each worke of Creation, and to make the litle world accord with the great. Practife this excercife, and add there vnto the praiers for euery day, which are fet downe in the end of this Booke.

Sunday. Which is the day, where on light was created, we fhould giue thanks to God, that he hath produced this teporall light, which is the fmile of heauen, and the ioy of the world, diftending it as a piece of cloth of gold

ouer

ouer the face of the Ayre, &
the Earth, and enkindling
it as a Torch wherewith to
behold his workes. Thence,
proceeding further, we will
giue him thankes, that he
hath afforded vs his fonne,
called by the Holy Fathers,
The Day-bringer, to communicate this great Light of
Faith vnto vs, which is as
faith S. Bernard) A Coppy
of the Eternity; we will hũ-
bly befeech him, this Light
may neuer be ecclipfed in
our vnderftandings, but may
daily more and more reple-
nifh vs with the knowledge
of his holy will. And for this
purpofe we muft heare the
word of God, & be prefent
at

at diuine seruice with al feruor, & piety. Carefully preserue your selfe from being
defiled through any disorder, on the day, which God
hath reserued to himself, &
frō giuing to Dagon the first
fruits of the weeke, which
you should offer vp at the
feete of the Arke of couenāt.

Monday. Which is the day,
wherin the Firmament was
created to seperate the cæle-
stiall waters, from the inferior & terrestriall; we will
represent vnto our selues,
that God hath giuen reason
vnto vs, as a Firmament to
seperate diuine cogitations
from animall; and we will
beseech him to mortify
anger

anger, and concupiscence in vs, and to graunt a perfect victory ouer all those Passions, vvhich oppose the law eternall.

Tuesday. The day vvherein the vvaters, vvhich did before couer the totall Element of the earth, were ranked in their places, and the earth appeared to become, the mansion, nourice, and tombe of man: We vvill figure vnto our selues the great vvorke of the Iustification of the World, made by the incarnate Word, when it tooke avvay a huge masse of obstacles, as vvell of ignorants, as sinne which couered the vvhole face of

the

the world, and raysed a
Church, vvhich appeared
as a blessed land, laden vvith
fruits and bevvtyes to edu-
cate vs in Faith, and bury vs
in the hope of a Resurrection. We vvill begg of him
to take avvay all the hin-
derances of our soule, to dis-
pell so many ignorances sinnes, imperfections, feares,
sorrovves, and cares, vvhich
keepe and drench it as in an
Abisse, and that he vvill replenish vs vvith the fruits
of Iustice.

Wednesday. In vvhich the
Sun, the moone, & the starres vvere created, vve vvill
propose vnto our selues for
obiect, the beyvty, & excel-
ency

lency of the Church of God,
adorned vvith the presence
of the Sauiour of the world
as vvith a Sun ; of the blessed Virgin, as a most resplendent Moone, and of so
many Saintes, which are as
starres of the Firmament;
& we will humbly begg of
God to embellish our soules
vvith Lightes, and vertues
suteable to its côdition. And
aboue all, that he vvould
giue vs the six qualities of
the Sun, Greatnesse, Beauty,
Measure, Feruor Promptnesse, and Fruitfullnesse.
Greatnesse, in the eleuation
of onr spirit aboue all things
created in a capacity of
heart, vvhich in neuer filled
led

led vvith any thing , but
God , Beauty in guifts of
grace , meafure , in the
power ouer our pafsion;
Feruor in excercifes of charity; Prõptneffe, in the obedience we ow to his law;
and Fruitfullneffe, in the
bringing forth of good
workes.

Thurfday, the day whereon
God (as faith S. Ambrofe)
drew Birds, & Fifhes out of
the waters. Birds to fly in
the aire, and Fifhes to abide
in this inferior Element ; we
will imagine with in our
felues the great feperation
that fhall be made, at the day
of Iudgmẽt, when of fo vaft
a number of men extracted
from

from one, and the fame
Maſſe ſome ſhall be rayſed
on high, to people heauen,
and enioy the ſight of God:
others, made a prey for hell,
and expoſed to euerlaſting
torments: And in this great
Abyſſe & terror of thoughts
we will beſeech God to hold
vs in the number of his E-
lect and afford vs the fauor
to make prooffe of our predeſtination, by our good, &
laudable Actions.

Friday. Whereon all o-
ther creatures were produced, and man was created,
who was from that time
appointed to be their Go-
uernour and King, we will
propoſe vnto ourſelues the
Greatneſſe

Greatnesse, Excellency and
Beauty of man in the talents
which God hath, giuen him
as well of Grace, as Nature;
what a thing it was to make
him, and that the hands of
the Creator were employed
in his production ; but how
much greater a mater it was
to repayre him it requiring
so much labour, so much
sweate and bloud of the
sonne of God, who anni-
hilated himselfe for him,
and so cherished, and foste-
red him (faith S. Thomas
in his treatise of Beatitude)
that he, who were not well
instructed by Faith, would
say : Man were the God, of
God himselfe. There vpon

I   we

we will begg that we may
not fruſtrate the merit of
the life of God , giuen to
eternize ours, and we will
practiſe ſome kind of Mortification , to beare God in
our Fleſh(as ſaith S.Paule)
and to conforme vs to the
ſufferings of the King of
the afflicted.

Saturday, Which is the
day whereon God reſted after the creatiō of the world,
we will meditate vpon the
repoſe which the beatifyed
ſoules enioy in heauen;
where there is no pouerty,
maladyes, ſorowes, cares,
calumnyes, perſecutions,
heate, cold, night, chaunge,
diſquiet, nor noyſe, The
body

body resteth fiue or six foote
within the earth , free from
the relapsing employments
of a life , fraile , & dying. It
is in the graue as in an inuin-
cible forteresse , where it
stands not in feare of debts,
sergeants , emprisonment,
fetters , and the soule when
it is glorifyed , liueth the
life of God himselfe , a life
vitall , a life louely , a life
inexhaustible, for which we
ought to sigh , take paines ,
and to begg it often of God
with teares in our eies, and
grones from our heart , as
saith S. Augustine.

It is necessary on the
same day to make a reuiew
of the whole weeke , to

examine the ſtate of your
ſoule, your paſſions, your
affections, your intentions,
ſcope, proceedings, and
progreſsions.

And eſpecially when the
moneth is ended, to con-
ſider diligently, what God
would haue of vs, what
we of him, and what courſe
we take to pleaſe both him,
and ourſelues : What de-
ſire we haue of perfection,
what obſtacles, what de-
fects, what reſiſtance, what
meanes, and to manage
all our endeauours vnder
the protection of the Saint
we take for our Patron in
the moneth following.

Deus-

Deuotion vpon the howers of the day, for such as are more contemplatiue, and lesse employed.

SECTION XII.

THE Church allso appointeth vs a practise of Deuotion, for all the howers of the day, if we will but make the application. It seemes to endeuour to make of a Christian Soldier, a true Bird of the Sun, which allmost euery hower saluteth this goodly starre, seeming by her song, and clapping of her winges, to

I 3   ap-

applaud it. It defireth that
in daily imitation thereof,
we loofe not fight of God,
and that we ftand in perpetuall fentinell to adore, and
worfhip him.

At the Breake of Day.

When the world feemes
to be borne with the day, it
inuiteth vs in the hymnes of
S. Ambrofe, to aske fiue
things, the protection of
God throughout the day,
Peace, Gouernment ouer
our fenfes, a Gard on our
heart, and mortification of
our Flesh.

In the progreßion of Day.
Which

Which is the hower, wherein the holy Ghoſt deſcended
in the forme of a fiery Tongue vpon the Apoſtles to
make them Doctors of the
vniuerſe, we begg of the
ſame ſpirit to repleniſh with
vigor & flames our vnder-
ſtandings, our wills, or Iud-
gements, our hearts, our tongues, and our mouthes, ſo
that we may enflame our
neighbours by our good
examples.

At Noone.

When the chieffe of ſtar-
res is in the midſt of his
courſe, we behold our Sun
of Iuſtice, to aske fower
I 4   things

things of him, to wit, alienation from the feruors of
Concupiscence, mortifica-
tion of choller, health of
body, and tranquility of
mind.

After Noone.

When the moity of the
carreere of day is paſt, and
that the Sun is allready de-
clining to the Weſt, we
caſt our ey vpon our great
Starre, and begg of him,
that as he is the immoueable Center about which
the whole world circum-
uolueth, and holds the beginning and progreſſion of
light in his handes, he will
graunt

graũt vs firſt happy veſpres,
ſecondly cõſtancy in vertue,
thirdly a good death.

In the Euening.

When darkneſſe approach-
eth we beſeech his diuine
maieſty to revnite our hearts
vnto him burthened by
ſinne, and vncollected by
ſuch diuerſity of actions,
that he will free them, and
prepare them for way of E-
ternity, to the end, we de-
priued of this temporall
light may make a ſweete
retreate into the boſome of
God, who is the fountaine
of the Lightes of vnderſtanding and that as we ending
our

our life, as we end the prefent day, may obtaine the triumph of Beatitude.

At the Shutting-in of Night.

When darkneffe allready couereth the face of the Earth, we will arraunge vs as litle Birds vnder the wing of God praying him that according to his cuftomary goodneffe, he will keepe vs vnder his protection, and driue away euill dreames, and nightly fantafies from our fleepe, ftaying the crafty furprizalls of our aduerfary, who roameth round about vs, as a roring lyon about the fheepfold.

Thefe deuotiós are graue,
fe-

serious , authentique , and able throughly to inſtruct a ſoule , which can practiſe them.

Now there being many who ſay our Ladyes Office, or their Beades at certaine howers of the day ? I will heere ſet them downe certaine conſiderations, which may ſtirre vp their douotiō.

An Excellent Practiſe for deuout ſoules which are affected to the office of our Lady.

Imagine with your ſelfe, that to ſay our Ladyes office is a ſeruice done to the moſt perfect of Gods creatures, applying the Howers of

of the day, to the principall
actions of her life, suffering,
and glorious, to enter into
her fauor, and protection,
by the imitation of her vertues.

At Matins, and Lawdes.

Matins, and Lawdes are
appointed to honour the
most pure Conception of
our Lady. There you shall
represent to your thoughts
a great Abysse of horror and
darknesse, which couereth
the face of the earth, and of
so many millions of soules,
which fall into their bodies,
as into the shadow of death,
abádoned to originall sinne:
But the soule of the most
blessed Virgin, preuented by

the

the aboundance of Gods
graces, is purifyed from this
great maſſe of corruption,
and rayſed into a ſphere of
radiace, where it ſeeth ſinne,
darkneſſe , and Death at its
feete.

At euery Pſalme you ſay,
you ſhall renew your attention , imagining with your
ſelfe , that totall Nature is
ſuſpended in admiration of
this great ſoule : That Heauen, the Elements , and all
creatures render to God immortall prayſes , for hauing
made ſo perfect a peice of
worke. In the Leſſons , you
ſhall ſee her in the boſome
of the Diuinity wholy ab-
ſorpt in its lights, where ſhe
repo-

reposeth as in a possession she acquired before all Ages, and you shall say vnto her with a heart full of loue, & confidence.

Ah! most adored Mistresse shall I honour a conception so pure with a heart so infected with earthly cotagion, and so poorely purged from worldly cogitations ! Ah what poore conceits, what wind , and what smoke! shall I neuer haue a strong conception of your vertues, to appropriate my selfe to you, and to conceyue *Iesus Christ* in the perfections of the most perfect of his Images.

At Prime.

As

At Prime which is the Spring of day, you shall represent to your mind the happy natiuity of your diuine Princesse, you shall see her arise as the dawning of day, vvhich whiteneth the heauens, gildeth the topps of moūtaines with its rayes, and diffuseth sensible sweetnesse throughout the bosome of totall Nature.

It will seeme vnto you that heauen smileth on her in all its mansions, that the earth dissolueth in reuerence vnder her feete, that all the patriarchs salute her, and all vertues crowne her. Haue you not a desire to say vnto her? Great Natiuity,

ty, which haſt made the
world to be borne againe, vi-
ctorious Miſtreſſe who haſt
diſſipated ſo many nights,
and cares by the firſt entrance thou maiſt into the
world, wilt thou not enter
into my heart, to take thēce
the veyle of ſo many ignorances which ouer clowd
the face of my ſoule, to
warme my tepidity, charme
my anxieties, and now vpon
this day to animate my actions by the power of thy
ſpirit. I am reſolued to be
borne to Grace in the conſideration of that day whe-
reon nature cauſed thee to
be borne to the world.

At

At the Third Hower.

The miſtery of the Preſentation ſhall be the entertaynment of your thoughts, you ſhall conſider this animated Temple, which moũteth vp to the inanimate, the Temple of IESVS, to the Temple of Salomon: What incẽſe, what perfumes, what victimes were preſented at the Sanctuary of the liuing God, and yet was all that nothing in cõpariſon of this diuine Virgin, who by her ſole preſẽtation accõpliſhed all thoſe offerings. Haue you not cauſe to ſay vnto her, O moſt louely daughter of the

K   Hea-

Heauenly Father, behold
the moſt captiue of thy ſer-
uants, who willingly offers
himſelfe to thy protection
to be preſented by thee to
thy well - beloued Sonne;
Take my heart, my deſires,
my prayers, & my workes,
I conſigne all I haue into
thy hands, there is nothing
ſo litle, which cannot become great, if it be recommended by thy merit, and
exalted by thy fauors.

At the ſixt bower.

The day which is in the
plenitude of lights ſetteth
before the bleſſed Virgin at
the height of her greatneſſe,
for

for you then shall behold
her in the Title of diuine
Maternity. You shall see an
Angell who in a deepe si-
lence treateth with her the
affaire of all Ages ; the mistery of the Incarnation. She
who was a Virgin by grace,
becomes a mother by mira-
cle, taking, that she was not,
yet not ceasing to be what
she was. The Word is in-
carnate in her bosome, as if
the whole sea should be
concluded in a Cockleshell;
she conceyueth by vertue,
she brings forth by miracle,
her flesh becomes the flesh
of the Sonne of God, & her
spirit diuinized thinkes on
nothing but extasies : Say

vnto her, moſt pure Virgin,
and incomparable Mother,
who can in thought equall
thy Greatneſſe , ſince God
himſelf, wholy infinite, hath
fownd the way to enlarge
himſelfe in ſome ſort in thy
ſoule, by dilating his lights
and bewtyes therein, and by
making himſelfe there to be
knowne , and acknowled-
ged as on the moſt eleuated
Throne of the world. If
thou beeſt the Queene of
Heauen through fauor, yet
thou faileſt not to be the
Mother of the whole earth
out of mercy; I implore
thy power to obtaine by
thee an entire participation
of his Graces , who made
him-

himfelfe wholy thine, to be
wholy ours.

At the ninth Hower.

The life, our Lady lead,
whilſt Ieſus was on the
Earth, ſhall be the excercize
of our conſideration. You
ſhall behold this diuine Mother, who becomes the inſeperable Companion of her
ſonne, and who followeth
him into Egipt, Iudęa, and
Galilee in ſeaſons the moſt
ſharpe, thorough wayes the
moſt yrkſome: All becomes
Roſes to her in the preſence
of her well-beloued, ſhe kiſ-
ſed his foot ſtepps, ſhe takes
part in his Trauells, ſhe
enchaſeth all his wordes,
K 3   as

as so many perles in her
heart, she adapteth her selfe
to all his actions, and her
heart perpetually moueth in
the heart of Iesus. O the
most faithfull of creatures
(you will say) and of mo-
thers the wisest; It is of thee
I will learne the art of true
loue. How many loues are
lost for being ill placed,
Take my heart, and turne
it towards the center of
thine, for I will loue all thou
louest, to possesse all thou
possessest : It is a portion,
which takes nothing from
thee, and which can make
all the world ritch with out
empouerishing thee, since
thy holy affections create
                        our

our gloryes, as thy consolations beget our Repose.

At Vespers.

This is the hower when
we should inter with the
blessed virgin Mother of
God into the three great
Abysses of the Passion
where you shall see a neglect
of Reputation, the paynes
of the mind, & the dolours
of body of our well beloued
Sauiour, you shall see him,
on a materiall Crosse, & the
Virgin on a spirituall where
loue piously witty in his
torments engraueth on her
heart out of an admirable
reflection all the woūdes of
her well beloued Dolorous

K 4 Mother

Mother) diuide thefe wou-
des with me, fince I made
thē I wil enter into thy fuf-
fering life, with all the extēt
of that meafure, which the
diuine Prouidence hath allotted my condition; why
should I be ashamed to be
the Daughter of fufferings,
fince thou haft made it thy
Trophey to be the mother
of Dolours.

At Compline.

You shall fixedly looke
on the happy end of your
holy Miftreffe, you shall obferue, how after the Refur-
rection, & Afcenfion of her
fonne, after thofe profufions
of the holy Ghoft, who was
fent

sent no comfort her, she
led a life, which held not of
Earth, but by very small
rootes of naturall necessi-
ties, but which perpertually
hung on the heart of God, a
life which wasted it selfe to
suffer euill, and do good,
obliging the whole world
without pretending any
other satisfaction then that
of her sonne, All the vertues
made stepps for her to
mount vp to the Throne of
her Assumption, her soule
wet to take the place which
was marked out for her,
fró the first day of her being
and her Body followed it,
since Purity had made he
winges of Glory, whic
walke

walked vpon death , as in a path of Immortaility. There it is where you shall say to her with admiratiō of heart: O what a Beginning of life what a progreſſion, & what an end! Mercyfull Mother, what ſhall I do, what ſhall I be amidſt ſo many embroylments, & ſuch chaunges of this mortall life? Aſſure me in the buſineſſe of my ſaluation , and graunt that at the day of my death I may happily finiſh the courſe of this life, to the end my laſt hower may for me be the firſt of my felicityes.

𝓐

A deuout Excercise to say the Beades by applying the Rose to the Rosary.

HAuing kissed the Crosse and adored the most holy Trinity in the first Bead, I figure vnto my selfe, that as it is called the Rosary, I should present a Rose vpon the Aultar of the Virgin, my singular Mistresse.

At the first Ten I consider that the Rose groweth among thornes, & our Lady amidst sufferings. For which cause I heartily say vnto her. Ah! most blessed Virgin thou art a rose among thornes, & I am to thee a thorne amidst thy Roses; wound vs with

with thy dolours, to cure vs
by thy comforts.

At the second, I note that
as the Rose-bud is enclosed
within its litle sheath, the
mother of God hath encha-
sed al the treasure of vertues
& glories in her profound
Humility and I say vnto
her, mistresse of the Hūble,
breake the pride of my
heart in the same manner,
as thou didst crush the head
of the Serpent.

At the third, I cōtemplate
the purple of the Rose,
which representeth vnto me
the Crosse of loue, and the
Martyrdome of the mind
of our Lady, and I will say
vnto her Princesse of Mar-
tyr:

:yrs, if I cannot yet become
ruddy with my bloud, let
me at leaft blush with the
shame of my finnes.

At the fowerth, I will ftay
vpõ the odour of the Queen
of flowers, and fay, fuch was
oh diuine Mary, that, of thy
vertues, giue me a pure foule
an innocent conuerfation,
which may cõtinually yield
a good odour to Ies' Chrift.

At the fift, I admire the
bewtie of the moft noble of
flowers, in the Incarnate of
her colour and in the excellent order of her leaues,
and fay, we number the leaues of the Rofe, (O moft
adorable Princeffe) but
who can recken vp the
Graces

Graces of thy foule, Take
pitty vpon mine, which
fhould not dare to appeare
fo black before thy bewty,
nor fo poore before thy riches.

At the fixt, I fay vnto my
felf, that as the Rofe is moft
wholefome for medecine,
the bleffed Virgin is foueraig-
ne for the cure of our maladies, and I with an humbled heart fay vnto her. Mercifull Lady, diffipate my
languors, cleanfe my woundes, I fhall thinke euen my
euills happy, if they may be
healed by thy hand.

Of

Of other Acts of Deuotion, and first of Masse.

SECTION XIII.

WE should heere Masse euery day, if it be possible, & at a certaine hower, and it is one of the principall Acts of Deuotion; the manner whereof ought to haue fiue conditions, *Consideration, Feruor, Decency, Example, Vnion*; Consideration for the vnderstanding; Feruor, for the will; Decency; for the Body, and exterior gestures; Example, for your neighbour; Vnion, for God.

God, *Confideration*, not to go thither by rote or out of complement, Hipocritically, or by constraint; but with attention, and reuerence, as to the Treasury of the suffering, and merits of Iesus Christ. *Feruor*, to pray there deuoutly, purely, and ardently, dismissing at that time the thought of all other affaires. *Decency*, in auoyding Tattle, ill postures, and the irreuerences of so many ill instructed people, who shall in the end find Gods vengeance in the propitiatory. *Example*, by edifying all there present, who ordinarily deriue notable apprehensions of God, from

from obseruation in the
Church of the deuotion of
persons of quality. *Vnion,*
in dilating your heart, and
soule in the heart and soule
of the sonne of God, by an
inward, and cordiall affection, hauing at that time neyther eares, eyes, nor thoughts, but for his loue; according to the saying of an auncient Father, who affirmed,
no man behaued himselfe
deuoutly enough in the
Church, if he thought there
were ought els in the world
then God, and himselfe;
It is much to the purpose
to haue good prayer boo-
kes, where the offices be
distinguished for euery day

L   of

of the weeke, and to say according to your them acleisure, and with a well rectifyed , and perseuerant piety.

A familiar, and well accommodated deuotion to heare Masse well, is to conforme your Action to that of this great Sacrifice.

Masse hath fiue principall partes. The first consisteth in the confession, & praise of God. The second in the instruction of the Epistle , the Ghospell and of the Creed. The third in Oblation. The fowerth in Confecration & consummation. The fift in Petitions and Prayers, which are most especially

pecially made at the latter
end. At the *Confiteor*, you shall
implore the diuine affiftáce,
to direct this Act well, you
shall confeffe your finns, &
confequently you shall giue
praife to God in the Hymne
of Angels, which is ordinarily repeated in this place
endeuouring to imitate the
reuerence of thofe Heauenly Quires.

At the Inftruction, if you
vnderftand not the wordes
of the Epiftle, and Ghofpell,
which is then read. Read,
and meditate attentiuely at
that time vpon fome fen-
tence of the fhort following
abridgemēt of the doctrine
of Iefus Chrift. It is a great

L 2   fpurre

spurre to perfection a litle
to taſt at leyſure the wordes
of our Sauiour, & it hath of-
times happened, that many
haue beene conuerted by a
good word, which deepely
penetrated their hearts.

---

*An Abridgment of the do-
ctrine of Ieſus Chriſt to
thinke vpon at the time
of Maſſe.*

SECTION XIIII.

AM the way, the trueth,
& the life : no man co-
mes to my heauenly Father,
but by me. *Iohn* 14.

The time is fullfilled, and
he Kingdome of God is at
hand

hand: do penance, & belieue in the Ghospell. *Marke* 1.

Come to me all yee that labour, & are burdned, and I will refresh you: Take vp my yoake vpon you, and learne of me, becaufe I am meeke, and humble of heart, and you shall find rest for your foules : For my yoake is fweete, & my burthen light. *Math.* 11.

All whatfoeuer you will that men do to you, do you likewife to them : For this is the law , and the Prophets. *Matth.* 7.

This is my precept, that you loue one another , as I loued you : Greater charity no man hath, then to dy for

L 3   his

his frends:you are my frēds,
if you do what I command
you. *Iohn.* 5.

Loue your enemies, do
good to them that hate you,
and pray for them who per-
secute and calumniate you,
that you may be the chil-
dren of your Father in heauen, who maketh the Sun
to rise vpon the good, and
the bad,and sendeth downe
his shower's on the iust, and
vniust. *Math.* 5.

Be mercifull as your hea-
uenly Father is mercifull:
Iudge no man , & you shall
not be iudged. Condemne
no man,and you shall not be
condemned : Forgiue, and
you shall be forgiuen: Giue,
and

and there shall be giuen to
you. *Luke 6.*

Take heed, & beware of all
auarice, for trāquility of life
consisteth not in aboūdance,
& large possessions. *Luke 12.*

Enter by the narow gate:
for wide is the gate, & large
is the way, that leadeth to
perdition, & many there are
who passe through it: but narow is the Gate, and straite
is the way which leadeth to
life, and few there are who
find it. *Math. 7.*

He who taketh not vp his
Crosse, and followes me, is
not worthy of me. *Math. 10.*

You shall be afflicted in
the world: but take courage,
I haue vāquished the world.
Iohn 19.   K 4   Be-

Behold I am with you all the dayes, euen to the end of the world. *Matth.* 28.

Watch, and pray that you may not fall into temptation. The spirit is prōpt, but the flesh is fraile. *Math.* 26.

Let your loynes be girt, and candles burning in your hands; and be yee like seruants who expect their Maister, returning from a feast; that when he comes, and knocketh at the gate, they may readily open it. *Luke* 12.

Take heed that your hearts be not ouer-charged with surfet, and drunkenesse, and the cares of this life. *Luke* 21.

The hower will come, when

when all such as are in their
Graues, shall heare the voice
of the sonne of God, & such
as haue done, well, shall
come to the resurrection of
life, but those who haue
done ill, to the resurrection
of Iudgment.

What is to be done at the Offer-
tory of Masse, and other
subsequent Actions.

SECTION XV,

AT the Offertory you
shall endeuor to stirre
vp in your selfe a great
reuerence of this incom-
parable

parable Maiefty, who com-
meth to repleniſh this Sacrifice with his preſence;
and you ſhall ſay : *My God,
diſpoſe me to offer vnto thee, the
merits of the life, and paſsion of
thy well-beloued Sonne. I, at this
preſent, in the vnion thereof make
oblation vnto thee of my vnderſtanding, my will , my memory,
my thoughts , my wordes my
workes, my ſufferings, my comforts, my good, my life, all that
I haue, all that I can, euer pretend vnto : and I offer it vnto
thee , as by the hand of the glorious Virgin Mary , and the
holy Angells, who are preſent
at this Sacrifice, to preſent vnto
thee the praiers of all this faithfull Company.*

After-

Afterward at the preface,
when the Priest inuiteth all
the people to lift their hearts vp to God, or when the
Angelicall Hymne is pro-
noūced, which is by the auncients called *Trifagion*, thefe
wordes may be faid, drawne
from the Liturgy of S. Ia-
mes, and S. Chryfoftome.

To thee the Creator of all
creatures vifible and inuifible: To thee the Treafure of
eternall bleffings : To thee
the fountaine of life , and
Immortallity : To thee the
abfolute Maifter of all the
world, be that praife , honour and worship yielded,
which thou deferueft

Let the Sun, the Moone,
the

the Quire of starres the Ayre, the Earth, the Sea, & all that is in the Celestiall, & Elementary world blesse thee. Let thy Hierusalem, thy Church from the first birth there of long since enrolled in Heauen, glorify thee. Let so many chosen soules of Apostles, Martyrs, and Prophets; Let Angells, Archangells, Thrones, Dominations, Principallityes, Powers, and Vertues : Let the dreadfull Cherubins, & Seraphins perpetually sing the Hymne of thy triumphs.

Holy, Holy, Holy, Lord God of Hoastes, Heauen & Earth are filled with thy Glory. Saueus, thou, who dost

doſt inhabit Heauen, which
is the pallace of thy maieſty.

After Conſecration at the Ado-
ration of the Hoaſt, Saint
Thomas ſayd.

MY Lord Ieſus, thou art
the King of Glory. Thou art
the ſonne of the eternall Father. It is thou, who, to redeeme the world haſt clothed thy ſelfe with our fleſh in
the wombe of a Virgin. It is
thou, who hauing ouercome
the agonies of death, didſt o-
pen heauen to vs. It is thou,
who ſitteſt at the right hand
of thy Eternall Father, and
who ſhalt iudge the liuing,
and the dead. My God helpe
thy ſeruãts whom thou haſt
redeemed

redeemed with thy most
pretious bloud.

---

*Hauing adored the Hoast, say
this prayer of saint Bernard
in his meditations vpon
the Passion.*

O Heauenly Father, be-
hold from thy Sanctu-
ary, and Throne of thy
Glory this venerable Hoast,
which is offered to the by
our Bishop, Iesus thy most
innocent, and sacred Sonne,
for the sinnes of his brethe-
ren, and let thy heart be soft-
ned notwithstanding the
multitude of our offences;
and miseries. Behold the
voice of the bloud of this
most

most innocent lambe which cryeth out to thee for mercy whilst he all crowned with glory, and honour standeth before thee at the right hand of thy maiesty. Looke (O God) on the face of thy Messias, who hath beene obedient to thee euen to death, & let not his sacred wounds be euer farre distant from thine eyes, nor the remembrance of the satisfaction he offered vnto thee for the remedy of our sinnes. O let all tongues prayse, and blesse thee in remembrance of the superaboundance of thy bounty. Thou who hast deliuered thine onely Sonne ouer to death vpon earth, to

make

make him our most faith-
full Aduocate in Heauen.

For Petition.

At our Lords Prayer, when
you haue said it repeate these
Words of the Liturgy heere
before alleaged.

My God remember our
holy Father, our Prelate, all
Pastors, and faithfull people
which abide in all the re-
giõs of the habitable world,
in the vnion of the Catholique Faith, & preserue them
in thy holy peace.

Good God, saue our most gra-
tious King, and his whole
Kingdome : Heare the prayers
which we offer for thy liuing
Image, vpon thine Aultars.

O

O God eternall, remember those who trauell by sea or land, and are exposed to so many dreadfull daungers. Remember so many poore pilgrims, prisoners, and exiles, who sigh vnder the miseries of the world.

My God remember the sick and all those who are in any discomfort of mind : Remember so many poore soules toyled out with acerbities, and afflictions, who implore thine assistance : Remember allso the conuersiō of so many Heretiques, Sinners, and Infidells, whom thou hast created to thine owne Image.

My God, remember our

M   Bene-

Benefactors and frends: Accept this great Sacrifice for the liuing and the dead, and graunt, that all may tast the effect of thy mercies; dissipate scandails, warres, and heresies, and afford vs thy peace and charity.

And at the end of Masse.

My God, powre downe thy graces vpon vs, direct our stepps in the pathes, fortify vs in the feare, confirme vs in thy frendship, & in the end giue vs the enheritance of thy children.

Of Confeſſion, an Aƈ of Deuo-
tion very neceſſary, with
aduiſe thereupon.

SECTION XVI.

I Ranke Confeſſion, and
Comunion among the de-
uotiõs of the weeke; For, in
ſuch as will lead a life pure,
it is not ſuperfluous if at
the end of euery weeke they
diſcharge themſelues of this
duty. And allthough I haue
ſpokē amply enough accor-
ding to my intention, of the
practiſe of thoſe exerciſes
in former Treatiſes which
I haue compiled thereof
M 2   and

and that it were, as to cary
a dropp of water into a Riuer, to handle it after so
great a plenty of writers :
yet I hold my selfe bound
out of the necessity of my
dessigne to tell you in few
wordes, that to make your
Confession good, it ought
to haue the qualityes of a
looking glasse. 1. *Solidity.*
2. *Liuely representation.* 3.
Clearenesse.

1. *Solidity*, in going to it
with much consideration of
your misery, of your sinnes
and imperfections.

2. Much reuerence towards
the Maiesty of God, who is
iudge in this Sacrament.

3. With a due, and serious
reuiew

reuiew of your conscience.
4. A distast of your offences, more for the offence done to God, then for any other consideration, stirring your selfe vp to the detestation of sinne. Because it being the capitall enemy of Iesus Christ, you haue lodged it in your heart. Because you haue reuiued that vvhich caused the author of life to dy. Because you haue repayed so many benefits of your Creator, with Ingratitude. Because you haue preferred caytiue & wretched pleasure before the glory of the liuing God, who is the source of all pleasures. Because you haue in your

M 3   selfe

selfe deſtroied his Image,
and Grace, to eſtabliſh the
power of Sathan.

5. It is neceſſary to endeuour a full accompliſhment
of the pennance enioined,
and a reall amendment.

Liuely repreſentation is made
by auoyding Confeſſions
made by rote, which haue
ſtill one & the ſame tenor,
or ſuch as are ouer dry, or
are not ſufficiétly vnfolded,
or thoſe which haue much
hiſtory in them, and are
cloyed with ſuperfluities.

By clearely repreſenting
the ſtate of your ſoule, and
ſuccinctly declaring how it
hath caryed it ſelfe.

If it be a generalll, or principall

cipall Confeſſion, eſpecially
of ſuch as haue liued in the
buſineſſes of the world; they
ſhall do well to run ouer the
explication of the Com-
mandements of God & the
Church, to ſee what they are
guilty of in them.

Then, *vpon the firſt* Com-
mandment, to examine ſin-
nes of Infidelity of con-
tempt of ſacred things, of
Impiety, of witchcraft, of
diuination, magick, ſuper-
ſtitiõ, diſtruſt of Gods mercy,
preſumption of ones owne
ability, Hipocriſy, and Sacri-
ledge in Gods ſeruice, telling
expreſſly vpon euery word,
in what, & how vpon what
motiue, & for what purpoſe.

Vpon the second, Oathes vvithout necessity, false othes, vowes violated, or not fullfilled, Blasphemies, Execrations, prophanation of holy things, and vvords of the scripture.

Vpon the third, Exercize of Husbandry, Traffick, Ciuill, and Criminall Iustice, and other vvorkes forbidden on Sundayes.

Irreuerence committed in vvholy loosing Masse, or some notable part of it, and in employing all your time in gourmandize, dauncings, bals, fopperies, and loose Libertinisme.

Vpon the fowrth, Cōtempt, Hatred, Distast, Ingratitude.

tude, Irreuerence and difo-
bedience tovvards Parents,
and Superiors, Negligence
tovvards fubiects, and houfhold feruants.

Vpon the fift; Enmities, quarells, violencies, treache-
ries, Iniuftice, oppreffion,
poifoning, abortions, mur-
thers, malice, outrages, and
cruelties committed againft
our neighbour. Ill treaty of
ones ovvne perfon by fome
anxiety, difpaire, or impatient defire of death.

Vpon the fixt, Fornication,
Adulterie, Inceft, vvhore-
dome, rauifhment, clande-
ftine Mariage, facrilege,
felfe-fofftneffe, pollution:
ill vfe of mariage, and other
M 2 infamous

infamous luxuries, vvhich *Tertullian* termeth monsters. Add all that vvhich makes vvay for impurity; dishonest thoughtes, vnchast wordes, wanton glaunces, kisses, touchings, Bookes, pictures, playes, loue-lettres, bals, Maskes, too free conuersation with euident daunger of sinne, and sometime charmes, drinkes, or other attractiues, characters, or sorceries.

Vpon the seauenth, Thefts, conniuence with Thieues, Falsification of instruments, Letters, Seales, Testaments, Contracts, Scedules, Bonds, false Bargaines, false Sales, false Money, Guiles, Vsurpation

pation of the goods of the Church, Simony, Vsury, Delay of due pyament, Iniustice, litigious Wrangling, lauish expence, Fowle play in game, cruelty towards the poore, and such like.

Vpon the eight, False witnesse-bearing, sollicitation of false witnesses, calunies, deramatory libells, lyes imposture, hipocrisy, dissimulation, flattery, treason, and dis-repute of a neighbour.

Vpon the ninth. Practises, & plottes against mariage, seducing the parties with wordes, signes, gestures, letters. guifts, attractiues, with deliberate purpose, and vnbrideled desire of sinne.

Vpon

Vpon the tenth. Inordinate couetise to become ritch, especially to the detriment of our neighbour.

Vpon the Commandements of the Church. Omissions of Masse, or great negligence, and distraction in hearing it on Festiualls commanded: sinnes against abstinence from meates, and Fastes appointed; against the vse of the Sacraments of Confession, & Cōmunion; against the obseruation of times for mariages; against integrity in the duty of Tythes.

In sinnes against the law of God, and the ordinances of the Church are cōprised the seauen sinns called mortall

tall and capitall. As against
the first Comandment, the
sinne of Pride, in a great opinion of ones selfe, obstinacy
in his owne iudgment, and
will, disobedience to Superiors, ambition of honour,
vanities, vaunts, and follies.
The sinne of sloth, in lazy-
nesse, or ill expence of time,
in neglect, and weaknesse of
courage, and in pusillanimity. The sinne of Gloutony,
in making a God of ones
belly. The sinne of Auarice,
vpon the seaueth. The sinne
of Anger, & Enuy vpon the
fift. The sinne of Luxury, v-
pon the sixt. See heere is
matter enough to examine
in a generall Confession. All

is

is propofed that may hap-
pen, This is not fpoken that
you fhould ftay vpon euery
poīt, Scrupuloufly to fearch
into that which neuer hath
beene. Confeffing often
you may examine your felfe
and confider your deport-
ments in a shorter method.

First in Acts of deuotion,
which more particularly
concerne diuine feruice, by
accufing ycur felfe of defects in the dues of Piety,
as Prayer, Maffe, examen of
Confcience, and other fuch
like of intentions leffe pure,
of negligences, irreueréces,
voluntary diftractions, con-
tēpt of things diuine, Faint-
neffe of Faith, and euill
                    thoughts

thoughts.

Secondly towards your felf in the direction of your interior, and exterior, namely in finnes of Vanity, Pride, Senfuality, Intemperance, Curiofity, Impurity, Idleneffe, Pufillanimity, Anger, Enuy, Iealoufy, Quarells, Auerfion, Impatience, Murmuring, Lyes, Detraction, Iniuries, Oathes, falfe promifes, Babble, Impertinent Tattle, Flattery, Flowtes, and mockery.

Thirdly, towards your neighbours, as well Superiors and equalls, as Inferiors, vnfolding the defects which may haue happened in the duty, which

which Charity or Iuſtice
oblige you to render to euery one according to his degree.

Examine euery one of
theſe heads & you ſhall find
matter of Confeſſion ; your
labour onely will be to reckon vp, ſpecify, & with all
circumſtance explicate your
faultes.

As for *Cleareneſſe* of Confeſſion it cõſiſteth in an vnfolding it ſelf in termes ſim-
ple, honeſt, and ſignificatiue.
They who cõfeſſe often may
be ſhort , onely ſpecifying
when they are ſleight things
ſeauen or eight articles, or
leſſe particularly happened
ſince their laſt Confeſſion.

S. Ber-

S. *Bernard* in the book of the interior Houſe, which is the Coſcience hath made a litle Forme of Confeſſion, cauſing the Penitēt to ſpeake in this manner to his Cōfeſſor.

Father, I accuſe my ſelfe, that I haue beene troubled with Anger, vexed with Enuy, puffed vp with Pride, & from thence haue contracted an inconſtancy of mind, vſed Tauntes, ſlaunders, and exorbitancy of tongue.

I accuſe my ſelfe, that I haue rather iudged my Superiors, then obeyed them, that being reprehended of my imperfections I haue murmured, and become refractory in my duty.

N   I ac-

I accuse my selfe to haue preferred me, before those who were better then I, vaunting, and publishing with much vanity and presumption, all which was mine, and despising other with scorne, and irrision.

I accuse my selfe to haue neglected the duty of my charge, and ambitiously pryed into others.

I neyther haue vsed reuerence in obedience, nor modesty in my wordes, nor order in my manners: Rather much obstinacy in my intentiõs, obduration in my heart, and Boasts in my discourse.

I accuse my selfe to haue played the Hypocrite, to haue

háue beene pertinacious in
hatred, & auerfion agaíſt my
neighbour, biting in words,
impatient of fubiection, am-
bitious of honour, couetous
of ritches, ſluggiſh in works
of deuotion & charity, litle
ſociable in conuerſation, &
& many times diſcourteous.

I accuſe my ſelfe to haue
beene ready to talke of o-
therfolkes actions, raſh in
cenſuring, contentious in
diſputing, diſdainfull in hearing, preſumptuous in re-
proouing others, profuſe in
laughter, *exceſſiue in pleaſures
of Taſt, and Game, ouer coſtly
in apparell*, Troubleſome to
my frends, clamorous agaíſt
ſuch as were peacefull,

vngratefull to thofe who did me good, harfh, and imperious to fuch as were vnder my charge.

I haue boafted to haue done that I did not, to haue feene what I faw not , to haue faid what I fpake not; and contrary wife I haue diffembled, and denyed to haue feene what I faw, and to haue faid what I fpake, and to haue done what I did.

I accufe my felfe of carnall thoughts, of impure remembráces of difhoneft apprehenfions, againft which I haue not made a ready refiftáce. One muft not thinke he can make a forme of Cófeffession, to be as a buskin for either legg. Consciences are like Faces, each one hath its diuersity, that which Saint Bernard speakes in generall may serue for direction, yet it must be particularized, & circumstantied, shewing the intention, the quality, the quantity, the manner, and continuance of a vice.

I will conclude with a manner of cōfession for soules which confesse often. The most exact accuse thēselues in particular of all distractions, ly:s, idle wordes, coldnesses, auersions, impatiencyes, and such like of which they tell the number, and it is very laudable,

N 3   but

but nothing necessary in ve-
niall sinnes, and Confessors
ought not importunately to
exact it, but leaue so many
good soules which liue very
purely to their owne way
when they are not reprehé-
sible, allthough they should
expresse their sinnes but in
very generall termes as thus.

I confesse to God, to the
blessed virgin Mary, to the
Angells, to all saintes, and
to you my spirituall Father,
To haue beene very cold in
my deuotions, to haue had
many distractions, irreue-
rencyes, and wandering of
mind in my prayers, which
I haue not couragiously
enough reiected.

To

To haue had some curious
glauncings , some impurs
thoughtes and imaginations
without consent , which I
not withstanding haue some
what negligently repelled.

To haue had vayne Com-
placencyes concerning my
selfe , vsing not intentions
pure enough in the seruice
of God , throughout all my
actions.

To haue had some sleight
auersions , iealousies, and
coldnesses, towards certaine
persons , shewing a con-
tempt of them, and other
affections not well ordered.

To haue freely spoken of
some slight defects, and imperfections of others , and

to haue passed my iudgment
vpon their actions, yet not
with any purpose to hurt
them.

To haue told some lyes,
spoken some wordes ouer-
freely, and sometimes allso
vaine, taunting and immo-
dest. To haue suffered my
selfe to be transported with
some motions of choller, &
impatiēce, which I haue not
speedily enough repressed.

To haue affected honour,
estimation, credit, contentment, and pleasure: to haue
been too sollicitous in worldly affaires, to haue taken
too much complacence in
good successes, to haue
beene too much discoura-
ged

ged in ill, sad, and pusilla-
nimous, and not hauing sufficient confidence in the Prouidence of God.

To haue beene too much
inclined to bodily ease, and
to Idlenesse, and litle to
haue regarded the perfec-
tion of my soule. Of these
sinnes, & of all other which
I haue committed, I ac-
cuse my selfe, and aske
Penance, and absolution.

An

An excellent prayer of S. Au-
gustine for the excercize of
Penance, taken out of a
manuscript of Car-
dinall Seripand.

SECTION XVII.

MY God, behold heere
the staines, and woūn-
des of my sinnes, which I
neither can, nor will hide
from the eies of thy maiesty.
I allready beare about me
the paine of them in the re-
morse of my conscience, &
in other sufferings & ordained me by thy Prouidence
for my correction, but I endure

dure nothing equiualent to
my demerit. One thing ama-
zeth me, that I so often feeling the payne of sinne, still
do retaine the malice, & obstinacy thereof. My weake-
nesse boweth vnder the burthen, & my iniquity is perpetually immoueable. My
life vapoureth away in languors and amendeth not in
its workes. If thou deferre
the punishment, I procra-
stinate my amendment, and
if thou chastice me, I cannot beare it. In time of correction I cofesse my offence,
& after thy visitation, I no
loger remeber my sorowes.
whilst thou hast the rod

in hand to scourge me, I promise all, but if thou with holdest it, I performe nothing. If thou touchest me, I cry out for mercy, and if thou dost pardon me, I againe prouoke thee to chastice me.

O my Lord God, I confesse my miseries vnto thee, and I implore thy clemency without which there is no saluation for me. My God, giue me that I aske of thee, allthough I deserue it not, since without any merit of mine, thou hast extracted me from nothing, to begg it of thee.

Of

Of Cõmunion which is the prin-
cipall of all the Acts of De-
uotion, with a short aduise
vpon the practise
thereof.

SECTION XVIII.

AS for your Cõmunion
remẽber the fix leaues
of the lilly it ought to haue:
I meane, Desire and Purity
before you present your self
there: Humility & Charity
in presenting your selfe
there; Thanksgiuing & re-
nouation of spirit after you
are there presented, It is fit
you endeauour from the
Ene

Eue of the day you communicate on, to make of your heart a fournace of desires, so that you may say with the Prophet Ieremy, *I feele a flaming fire in my heart, which spreadeth it-selfe into my bones and so great is the violence thereof, that I am not able to endure it.* Let vs go to this holy Table, as the thirsty Hart to the Current of waters, as a hungry man to a feast, as the Bridegrome to his a thousand times wished wedding, as the couetous man to a mine of God, and a Conqueror to spoiles, and let there be need of any spurre to our desires, since,

there,

there, is our beginning,
our originall, our Trea-
sure, and soueraigne Good?
As for purity, I speake
not of that, which con-
cerneth the purgation of
mortall finnes, by Confes-
fion, which is wholy ne-
ceffary, and which can not
be omitted without facri-
ledge : I speake of a more
particular purity, which
consisteth in faith, in affections, and intentions.

On the day of com-
municating haften in the
morning to this heauenly
Manna : Entertaine not
your selfe ouer much in
the decking vp of your
body, nor in diffusing
your

your spirit in vayne affaires:
but keepe the veſſell of your
heart, as a pot well ſtop-
ped to powre it out at the
Table of your ſpouſe. It is
at that inſtant when you
ſhould imitate the ſeraphins
of the Prophet Eſay, and
hold all your wings ſtill, but
two, which are humility, &
charity; For theſe are the
two wigs, which you ſhould
nimbly fanne. Firſt by pow-
ring your ſelfe out in reuerence before the eyes of this
ineffable Maieſty by lowly
abaſing your ſelfe to the
center of your nothing, by
ſubduing all preſumptions,
vanityes, and fopperies,
thorough a moſt perfect humility

mility of spirit. Secondly by
stirring vp liuely, and ardent
affections, with all the endeuour of your heart, and if
that suffice not, offer all to
God, in the vnion of his o-
nely Sonne, and the merits
of his most blessed Mo-
ther.

After Communion you
must stay vpon the two last
leaues of the Lilly: which
are Thankfgiuing, and renouation of spirit. You then
must adore this great
Gueast, which you haue in
your heart, as if you were
some petty parcell of the
great harmony of the
world.

To offer the whole vni-

uerſe vnto God, as a Table
hãgd on his auītar, collected
in the perfectiõs of his onely
ſonne, who is wholy yours,
being ſo liberally giuen vnto
you, ſo ſolemnly, and ſo ir-
reuocably, as he whoſe Diuinity, ſoule, life, fleſh, and
bloud you receiue in this in-
comprehenſible Sacrament.

To giue him thankes for
the infinits riches he hath
conferred on the ſacred hu-
manity which you enioy, &
for that he hath afforded
you his ſonne for Father,
for Maiſter, for Head, and
Redeemer. For the bleſſings
he hath communicated to
all the faithfull by the helpe
of this fountaine of inex-
hauſti-

nauftible Grace, for the fpe-
ciall fauors he hath done
both to you, and others, for
the naturall Talents with
which he hath honoured
you, yea allfo for the viciffi-
tude of confolations , and
defolations with which he
enterlaceth your life. Laftly
for the prefent vifitation he
hath made in your fo ill
prepared heart.

After Adoration, & Thākf-
giuing followeth petitiō for
the faithfull & infidels whofe conuerfion we fhould de-
fire:for the Church, our holy Father, & all the Prelates
which gouerne it , namely
him who is our Paftor. For
the perfon of the king & the

O 2   whole

whole Kingdome, for our
Allyes, frends and benefactors both liuing and dead.
It is good to begg for ones
selfe those seauen guifts
which a holy Virgin (as
writeth *S. Bonauenture*) dayly
asked of God. 1. Efficacious
grace to fullfill the law of
loue. 2 To loue all God loueth. 3 To hate al he hateth.
4. The guift of Humility, of
Chastity, Obedience, Con-
tempt of the world, and the
adornement of all vertues. 5.
That God would make his
true Temple of our soule &
body. 6. That he would giue
vs his vision in Beatitude. 7.
That he may worthily be
serued in this place where
　　　　　　　you

you communicate, and in all
other parts of Chriſtēdome.
To conclude all with a renouation of the oth of Fidelity, which we haue made
to our great Maiſter, and
more reſolutely then euer to
bēd our ſelues to his ſeruice.
And ſince we are vpon the
palme let vs gather the
fruits, which are ſpirituall
food, ſtrength againſt temptations, heauenly alacrity,
light of vnderſtanding, Flames of Charity, great vnion
with God, Encreaſe of vertues, Hope of our Glory,
renouation in all our faculties and functions, and particularly let vs euer ſtay
vpon ſome peculiar obiect

O 3   of

of vertue, which we craue
of our Gueſt in fauor of this
celeſtiall viſitation.

Now if you deſire to
know the Qualities which
will make you diſcerne a
luke-warme Communion
from a feruent, I ſay, a good
Communion ought to be,
*Light-ſome, Taſtfull, Nutritiue,
Effectuall. Light ſome*, in illu-
ſtrating you daily more
and more with reſlections,
and verities of Faith, which
may tranſport you to the
eſtimation of things diuine,
and to the contempt of
wordly, fraile, and tempo-
rary.

Taſtfull, in making you
relliſh in will, and ſence,
what

what you know by the light
of vnderstanding. But if you
haue not this Taftfullnesse
in a deuotion tender, & sensible, wonder not at it : For
sensible deuotion will many
times happen to him, who
hath lesse charity, as it is obserued by the great Doctor
Richardus vpon the Canti-
cles : *Affectuosa dilectio in-
terdum afficit, minus diligen-
tem.* It is enough that you
haue in the vpper region of
your soule good Habits of
vertue. *Nutritiue,* in keeping
your selfe in a good spirituall way, in good thoughts
of heauenly things, good affections towards the seruice
of God, free from drynesse,

meagernesse, and voluntary
sterility. *Efficacious*, in applying your self instantly to
the excercise of solid vertues, Humility, Patience,
Charity, & to the workes of
mercy. For that is the most
vndoubted signe of a good
Communion.

It is good to present your
selfe in it with sincere intentions, well pondered, and
adapted to occasions, as S.
Bonauenture obserueth in
the Treatise he wrot vpon
preparations for Masse, one
while communicating for
remission of your sinnes, a-
nother while for the remedy
of infirmities, sometimes
for deliuerance from some
affliction,

afflictiõ, another time to obtaine a benefit, one while for
a Thankf-giuing, another
while for the helpe of your
neighbour, & aboue all for
the foules in Purgatory.
Laftly to offer perfect praife
to the bleffed Trinity, to re-
cord the fufferings of Iefus
Chrift, and daily to encreafe
in his loue. For this purpofe
you fhall fay before com-
municating this prayer of
great S. Thomas.

O moft fweet Iefus, my
Lord, and Maifter, let the
power of thy loue, more pe-
netrating then fire, & more
fweete then honey, drench
my heart in the Abyffe of
thy mercyes, pulling it frõ
in

inordinate affections of all
things vnder heauen, that I
may dy in thy loue, since
out of loue thou hast vou-
chsafed to dy for me on the
crosse.

Then.

O God eternall, and om-
nipotēt, Behold I approach
to the Sacrament of thy onely sonne my Lord Iesus
Christ. I come thither as
the sick to the Phisitian, as
the defiled to the fountaine,
as the blind to the light of
eternall splendor, as the
poore to the Lord of hea-
uen and earth, as the naked
to the King of glory. I therefore (o Lord) hūbly beseech thy goodnesse, & infinite

nite mercy to cure my ma-
lady, to cleanse my pollu-
tions, to enlighten my blindnesse, to enritch my pouerty,
and cloth my nakednesse,
that by this meanes I may
receiue the bread of Angels,
the King of Kings, the Lord
of Lords with as much re-
uerence, feare, and sorow
for my sinnes, with as much
faith and purity, good intention, and humility, as is
necessary and fit for the saluation of my soule.

Graunt (O Lord) that
I may not onely receiue the
Sacrament, but he vertue &
grace also of the Sacrament.
Graunt (O most benigne
Father) that receiuing
thy

thy onely Sonne, veiled, and couered in this life, I may see him without vaile & couerture in the other life, in which he liueth & raigneth with thee for euer.

And after Communion, say.

O the God of peace and loue, do you vouchsafe so much to descend? It is to be humbled, beyond the Cribb of Bethleem to enter into so caytiue and miserable a heart as mine. Most Gracious Lord I prostrate my selfe in heart and affection before the Abysses of thy great, and diuine mercy, & hauing not wordes sufficient to expresse my thoughts, I reuerence thee with a

chast

chaſt ſilence.

O let Heauen in all its ſe-
nerall Quires bleſſe thee, &
thanke thee for thy eternall
Charity, my ſweete, & moſt
mighty Maiſter; and ſince I
muſt bow vnder thy great-
neſſe, let me diſſolue, & be
annihilated in thy heart: For
I will no lõger be any thing,
then what I-ſhall be in the
ſoule of Ieſ⁹, where all good
ſoules liue, all vnderſtan-
dings are enlightned, all ſacred loues breath, and all
liues are Deifyed.

Looke not on my ſinnes,
but behold thy Church, in
the boſome whereof I haue
approached to thee. Suffer
not that this ſacramēt which
thou

thou haft inftituted for my
fanctification may to d y
become my iudgment, and
condemnation: but buckler
and defence , ornament ,
peace, and totall felicity.

O my Redeemer raigne
hereafter in my heart as a
King, rule there as a Lord,
Teach it as a Maifter, gouerne it as a father, comfort
it as a frend, support it as a
brother, loue it as a Spoufe.
O moft fweet Gueft of my
foule, who art the repofe of
labours , the refrefhment of
ardours, and folace of mife-
ries, wafh cleane in me what
is defiled, moifte what is dry
cure what is infirme, & bow
that which refifteth thy wil.

Confe-

Consequently make these pe-
titions of Saint
Augustine.

O God let me know thee,
& let me likewise know my
selfe, and let there where
thou art, euer be the scope
of my desires. O God let me
haue no hatred but for my
selfe, nor loue but for thee:
Be thou the beginning, the
progresse and end of all my
actions.   My God graunt
me to humble my selfe euen
to the deepest Abysses, and
to exalt thee aboue the
Heauens, hauing my heart
wholy emploied in thy prai-
ses. My God let me dy in
my

my selfe, let me liue in thy
heart, and let me accept all
which shall come to me
from thy Prouidence, as
presents from heauen. My
God, let me pursue my selfe
as an enemy, & follow thee
as a singular frend. My
God, let me haue no other
assurance, then the feare of
thy name nor confidence
then distrust of my selfe. My
God, when will the day
come that thou wilt lift vp
the veyle of the Temple, &
graunt me to behold thee
face to face, and to enioy
thee for all eternity?

THE

THE SECOND
PART OF THE
DIVRNALL.

Of Acts of Vertue.

SECTION I.

*Twelue fundamentall Consider-
tions of Vertues which may be
read ouer euery Moneth.*

YOu must be fully
perswaded, that the
chieffest deuotion
consisteth in the practise of
good workes, without w-
hich there is neither solid
piety, nor hope of saluation.

P   Heauen

Heauen hath none but blessed soules in it, and Hell is filled with wicked. But the world where in we liue hath diuers sorts of merchants; some trafick in Babylon, other in Sion: some through their ill trade, and disorder of their actions insensibly hasten to the vtmost misery, which is a seperation from the life of God in an eternity of Torment. Other tend directly to the prime, and Soueraigne Happinesse, which is the vision, fruition, and possession of God in a perpetuity of inexplicable contentmens. If you desire to take this way, I counsell you to set oftentimes before
your

your eyes thefe twelue confiderations, which I haue in-
ferted in the Holy Court:
For thefe in my opinion are
twelue great motiues to all
the Actions of vertue.

The firft is the nature, and
dignity of man, to wit, that
the firft and cōtinuall ftudy,
and endeuor of man fhould
be man himfelfe ; To fee,
what he hath beene, what
he is and what he fhall be:
what he hath beene, no-
thing; what he is, a reafonable creature ; what he fhall
be, a Gueft of Heauen, or
Hell, of an eternall felicity,
or of an euerlafting vnhap-
pineffe.

What he is according to
P 2   Nature

Nature; a Maister-piece,
where many prerogatiues
meete together; a body cō-
posed of an admirable Ar-
chitecture; A soule endowed
with vnderstanding, Rea-
son, with Iudgment, will,
memory, Imaginations and
opinions; A soule, which in
an instant flyeth from one
Pole to the other, descen-
deth euen into the center of
the world, and mounteth vp
to the Topp; which is in an
instāt in a thousand seuerall
places, which embraceth
the vvhole world without
touching it, which goeth,
which passeth, which brea-
keth through, which diues
into all the Treasuries, and
maga-

magazins of nature, which
findeth out all fortes of In-
uentions, which inuenteth
artes , which gouerneth
commonwealths, and pene-
trateth worldes. In the meane time this foule feeth
about it felfe an infinite
number of dogges that
barke at its Happineffe, and
endeuor to bite it on all
fides.

Loue fooleth it , ambition
turmoyleth it, auarice ru-
fteth it , defires and luftes
enflame it, vayne hopes flatter it, pleafures melt it, def-
paires depreffe it , choller
burnes it, Hatred exafpera-
teth it, enuy gnaweth it, iealoufy pricketh it , reuenge

enra-

enrageth it, cruelty vnciui-
lizeth it, Feare frosteth it,
and sadnesse consumeth it.
This poore soule shut vp in
the body, as a Bird of Paradice in a cage, is alltogether
amazed, to see it selfe assay-
led by all this mutinous multitude, and allthough it haue
a scepter in hand to rule, it
not withstanding suffereth
it selfe to be haled away, &
dragged along into a miserable seruitude.

Consider likewise, what
man is, through sinne; vanity, weaknesse, incostancy,
misery, and malediction.

What he becommeth by
Grace; a child of light, a
terrestriall Angell, the sonne
of

of a celestiall Father by a-
doption, brother & coheire
of Iesus Christ, a veffell of
Election, the Temple of
the holy Ghost.

What he may arriue vnto
by Glory, to be an inhabi-
tant of heauen, who shall
see the starres vnder his
feete, which he hath ouer
his head, & who shall be filled with the sight of God,
His, beginning, his End, his
reall, onely, and originall
Happinesse.

Secondly, the benefits receyued from God conside-
red in generall, as those of
creation, conseruation, Redemption, vocation, and in
particular the guifts of the

Body, of the soule, of nature, capacity, ability, industry, dexterity, Fore sight, nobility, offices, authority, meanes, credit, reputation, good successe of affaires, & such like which are giuen vs from heauen, as instruments to worke our saluation. And sometimes one of the greatest blessings, is that (which few esteeme a blessing) not to haue these benefits, which lead a presumptuous, haughty, weake, and wordly spirit into a head-long precipice; nay contrary worldly aduersities put him into the estimation of heauenly. things. Man seeing what he hath beene, what

what he is , what he muſt
become , from whence he
comes , whither he goeth,
and how the vnion with
God , his Beginning , is his
Butt, ſcope and ayme : If he
do that which Reaſon di-
ƈateth , he then inſtantly
takes a reſolution to haue
neither , nerue , veine , nor
artery which tendeth not
to his end, to vanquiſh his
paſſions , and no further to
make vſe of creatures , but
ſo farre forth , as he ſhall
know them profitable to
lead him to his Creator.
Euery Creature ſpeaketh
theſe words to man, O man
keepe what is giuen thee,
expeƈt what is promiſed
thee

thee, and auoyd what is forbidden thee.

The third Consideration is the Passion of the sonne of God, an Abysse of dolours, scornes, annihilations, loue, mercy, wisdome, humility, patience, charity. The Booke of Bookes, the science of sciences, the secret of secrets, the shopp where all good resolutions are forged, where all vertues are purifyed, where all the Knotts of holy obligations are tyed. The schoole where all Martyrs, all Confessors, and all Saints are made. Our faintnesse, our weaknesse onely proceeds from the want of

behol-

beholding this excellent figure. Who euer would
complaine of doing too
much , of suffering too
much , of being too much
abased, too much despised,
too much turmoyled , did
he but consider the life of
God deliuered ouer and a-
bandoned for him to so
many panifull labours , so
horrible affronts , and so insupportable torments ? O
God , O my wounded
God ! As long as I shall see
thy woundes , I will neuer
liue without wound , sayd
S. Bonauenture.

The fowrth, the examples
of all Saints, who haue walked in the Royall way of
the

the Croſſe: When we conſider the progreſſion of Chri-
ſtianity, the long ſucceſſion
of ſo many Ages, whereſoe-
uer our cõſideration reſteth
it findeth nothing but the
bloud of Martyrs, combats
of Virgins, praiers, teares, fa-
ſtings, ſackcloth, Haire cloth
perſecutiõs, afflictions of ſo
many Saintes, who haue (as
it were) wonne heauen by
maine force. Such there
haue beene, who had allready filled Sepulchers with
their members thorne with
engines, and ſwords of per-
ſecution, and yet ſuruiued
to endure; and ſuffer in their
bodyes, which had more
woundes, then partes of
body

body to be tormented, Is it
not a shame to haue the
same name, the same Ba-
ptisme, the same profession,
and yet to be desirous perpetually to tread on Roses;
to be embarqued in the great
vessell of Christianity with
so many braue spirits, which
euen at this day worke
wonders in the world, and
yet to go vnder hatches to
sleepe in the bottome of the
shipp, as needlesse creatures, outcastes, and the very
scornes of reasonable na-
ture.

The fift, the peace of a
good conscience (the in-
seperable companion of
good men) which sugreth
all

all their sharpneſſe, and ſea-
ſoneth all their acerbityes.
A perpetuall banquet, a por-
tatiue Theater, a delicious
Torrent of inexplicable
contentments, which begin
in this life, and which many
times are felt among chaines, empriſonments, and
perſecutions. What will it
be when the conſumma-
tion ſhall be made in the
other world, when the Curtaine of the great Tabernacle ſhall be drawne aſide,
when we ſhall behold God
face to face, in a Body im-
paſſible as an Angell, ſub-
tile as a Ray of light, ſwift
as the wings of thunder,
radiant as the Sun, and
that

that he shall be seene in so
goodly and flourishing a
company , in a pallace of
ineſtimable glory,and when
one ſhall leade no other life
but the life of God , of the
knowledge of God , of the
loue of God, as long as God
ſhall be God ? What will
this life be , nay what will
this life not be ; ſince all
bleſſing eyther are not, or
are in ſuch a life , of light
which place cannot cōpre-
hend; of voyces and harmo-
nies which time cānot take
from vs;of odours which are
neuer waſted ; a feaſt which
neuer is finiſhed ; a bleſſing which well may eter-
nity giue , but of which it
neuer

neuer ſhall ſee an end.

The ſixt, It is on the other ſide to be conſidered the cōdition of this preſent life, a True dreame, which hath the vnquietniſſe of ſleepe, neuer the repoſe; a childiſh amuſement, a Toyle, of burthenſome, and euer relapſing actions, where for one roſe a thouſand thornes are fownd, for one ownce of honey a Tun of gall, for bleſſings in appaⁿrance, euills in ſubſtance. The moſt happy count their yeares, and cannot reckon their grieffes. The Carreerers of the greateſt honours are all of Ice, and moſt times are bownded
.with

with headlong ruines. The
Felicities thereof are floating Ilands, which allwaies
recule backward when we
thinke to touch them with a
finger. They are the feasts of
Heliogabalus, where there
are many inuitations, many
ceremonies, many reuerēn-
cies, many seruices, & in conclusion we find a Table & a
Banquet of . waxe , which
melts before the fire , and
from thēce we returne more
hungry then we came. It is
the enchaunted egg of Oro-
mazes wherein this Impo-
stor vaunted he had enclosed all the happinesse of the
world , and breaking it
there was nothing to be

Q   found

found but wind. All thefe
pleafures flatter our fenfes
with an impofture of falfe
colours : why do we fuffer
thofe eyes to be taken in
the fnares of error, which
are giuen to vs by heauen
to behold the light, and not
to ferue falfhood ? Yea that
which fhould greatly di-
ftaft vs in this prefent life,
is that we liue in an Age
ftuffed with maladyes , as
old age with indifpofitions.
We liue in a world greatly
corrupted , which may be
faid, to be a monfter, whofe
vnderftanding is a Pit of
darkneffe; Reafon, a fhopp
of malice ; will, a Hell
where a thoufand paffions
                    outra-

outragiously raigne ; Its
eyes are two channells of
fire, from whence fly sparkles of Concupiscence;
Its tongue is an instrument
of malediction ; visage,
a painted Hypocrisy; Body
a Spunge of Ordures:
Hands, the Tallons of Harpyes ; and finally it seemeth to haue no other faith,
but Infidelity; no law, but
proper passion : no God
but its owne belley ; what
content can there be to liue
with such a monster ?

The seauenth, If there be
pleasures in life , they do
nothing but a litle sleightly ouerflow the heart with
a superficiall delectation,

Q 2   Sadnesse

Sadnesse diueth into the bottome of our soule, and when it is there, you may truely say, it hath leaden feete, neuer to forsake the place: But pleasure doth onely sooth vs in the exterior partes, and all those sweete waters runne downe with full speed into the salt sea, which was the cause why S. Augustine said that when any prosperity presented it selfe to him, he durst not touch it. He looked on pleasure, as on a fleeting Bird, which seemes willing to entertaine you but flyes away when your are ready to lay hold on her.

The

The eyght; Pleasures are
conceyued in the senses, and
like Abortiues are consu-
med in their Birth. Their
desire is full of disturban-
ces, their accesse is of violent, forced, and turbulent
agitations : Their satiety is
forced vvith shame, and
repentance : They passe
avvay after they haue vvea-
ried the body, and leaue it
like a Bunch of Grapes,
vvhence the juice is extracted by the vvine-presse, as
saith S. Bernard: They last
as long as they can: but must
end vvith life, and it is a
great chaunce, If during
life they serue not their
Host for an Executioner. I

Q 3   see

see no greater pleasure in the vvorld, then the contempt of pleasure.

The ninth; Man vvhich vvasteth his time in pleasures, vvhen they are slipped avvay much like vvaters engendred by a storme, findeth himselfe abandoned, as away-farer dispoiled by a Thieffe : So many golden Haruests vvhich time presented him are passed, and the rust of a heauy, and vn-wieldy age furnisheth him with nought but thornes, sorowes to haue done ill, and inabilities of doing well: what then remaineth to be said; but that which the miserable King spake, who for

a

a glaſſe of water gaue his
Scepter: *Alas! muſt I for ſo
short a pleaſure, looſe ſo great
a Kingdome!*

The tenth: Euill alwayes
beareth ſorrow behind it:
but not alwayes true pen-
nance. It is a moſt par-
ticular fauor of God, to
haue time to bemone the
ſinnes of our paſſed life,
and to take Occaſion by
the fore-lock. Many are
packed away into the o-
ther world, without euer
hauing thought of their
paſſage, and ſuch there are
that ſuppoſe they ſhall haue
many teares at their death,
who will not haue one good
Act of repentance: They
bewayle

bewayle the sinnes which
forsake them, and not God
whom they haue lost. True
contrition is a hard piece
of worke. How can he me-
rit it, who willingly hath
euer demerited?

The eleauenth : In the
meane time death comes a
pace; It expecteth vs at all
howers, in all places ; and
yet you cannot thinke of it
one sole minute, so much
the thought thereof displea-
seth you. The summons
of it are more cleare and
perspicuous then if they
were written with the bea-
mes of the Sun , and yet
we can not read them : Its
Trompet perpetually sown-
det \>

deth more intelligibly then
Thunder, and we heare it
not. It is no wonder that
Dauid in the 48th. Pfalme
calleth it an Ænigma ac-
cording to the Hebrew: E-
uery one lookes vpon the
figure, and few vnderftand
it notwithftanding it is a
cafe côcluded we muft take
a long fare well from all
things which appertaine to
life, which can be exten-
ded no further, then life
it-felfe: and it is a cafe re-
folued, that ferpents and
wormes muft be enherited
in a houfe of darkneffe. It
is a goodly leffon, who fo
euer can well learne it. To
know it well once, it muft
euery

euery day be ſtudyed, we in euery place ſee watches, clocks, and dyalls ſome of gold, ſome of ſiluer, and others enchaſed with pretious ſtones: They aduertiſe vs of all the howers, but of that which muſt be our laſt, and ſince they cannot ſtrike that Hower, we muſt make it ſownd in our owne Conſciences. At the very inſtant, when you read this a thouſand, and a thouſand perhaps, of ſoules vnloſened from the body, are preſented before the Tribunall of God, what would you do if you now preſently were to beare them company? There is but one thing

to

to be said , Timely dispise
in your body the things of
which you shall haue no
need, out of your body.

The twelfth , your soule
shall go out , and of all at-
tendants of life shall haue
none , but good and bad by
its side. If it be surprized in
mortall sinne, Hell shall be
its share; Hell the great lake
of the anger of God; Hell,
the common sewer of all the
ordures of the world; Hell,
the store-house of eternall
fire; Hell , a depth without
bottome ; where there is no
euill but may be looked for,
nor good which may be ho-
ped.

What shall one do , who
goeth

goeth out of greatneſſe, and
worldly delights, to enter
into ſuch a priſon, where he
muſt be clothed with flames,
liue on the gall of Dragons,
ly on burning colles, ſee no
faces but of diuells and the
damned, by the light of the
fire of his owne torments:
Heare nought but enraged
yells, ſmell nought but pla-
gues and poyſons, and
toutch nothing but paine?
And what a deſpaire will
there be, when one thin-
kes, that a million of paſſed ages ſhortneth not a moment of ſo horrible tortures, and that the greateſt
miſeries begin perpetually,
without euer ending? and
vvhich

which is more, that in the loffe of all things, one cannot loofe the memory of a God loft?

Is not that man infinitely fenceleffe, who fetteth not his cofcience in order, whilft the light of God reflecteth yet on his head, and that he hath the power of his owne faluation in his hands?

Thefe twelue Confiderations are likewife very proper to meditate on euery Moneth, at leyfure.

Seauen pathes of Eternity, which
conduct the soule to
great vertues.

For the Contemplatiue.

SECTION II.

THese twelue Conside-
rations well weighed,
cause vs to take a serious
resolution to dispose vs per-
fectly to good, whereof, If
you desire some demonstra-
tion, obserue, that Saint Bonauenture as with a finger
pointeth vs out seauen
broad wayes, and seauen
large

large gates, which leade vs
directly to this most happy
Eternity : and I heartily
wish we had as much cou-
rage to follow them, as he
had grace to vnfold them.

First, that the beginning
of your vertues, and felicityes consisteth in the knowledge of God, and the condition of the other life, of
which one cannot be igno-
rant without some crime, &
which is neuer vnderstood,
without much profit ; you
must know, the first Gate
of Eternity, is, to haue good
& sincere intentiōs towards
things eternall : To conceiue
a strong resolution to procure your saluation vpon
any

any price, euer to hold things
temporall as fleeting Birds,
which looke vpon vs from
the braunch of a tree, and
afford vs some sleight war-
ble, and instantly fly away.
To thinke, that to haue a
vicious soule, in a splendid,
and glorious accoustrement
of fortune, is to haue a leaden blade, in an iuory scab-
bard.

To banish through out
the whole course of your
life, and excercise of charges, intentions euill, hypo-
criticall, impure, mercena-
ry; To tend God, to do for
God, to intend the honour,
and glory of God aboue all
things.

You

You shall make no slight
progreſſion, if you will tread
this path. From thence you
shall come to the second,
which is the meditation of
things eternall, wherein the
Kingly Prophet exerciſed
himſelfe, like a braue cham-
pion, when he ſaid, *I haue*
conſidered elder dayes, and haue
ſet before the eyes of my ſoule
yeares euerlaſting. The good
intention you shall conceiue
to proceed to Eternity, will
daily impreſſe your thoughts
with a God eternall, a Heauen eternall, a Hell eternall,
a life euerlaſting. And as
the Ewes of Iacob by loo-
king on the party-colou-
red wands brought forth

R diuer-

diuersifyed lambes : so by
considering and beholding
Eternity , all your actions
vvill , be coloured vvith
Eternity. And if some temporall pleasure be presented
vnto you , or any accomo-
dation of fortune to com-
mit a sinne , you vvill say
that vvhich the Orator De-
mosthenes did of the bevv-
tifull Lais , vvhen a huge
summe of money vvas as-
ked him to see her : *I will
not buy repentance at such a
rate* ; I am not so bad a
merchant , as to sell the e-
ternall for the temporall.

Hauing passed through
this Gate , you shall come
to the third , vvhich is the
Gate

Gate of light , called *Con-*
templation of eternall things.
There you fee things di-
uine , not onely by vvay of
argument and difcourfe , as
an accompt , or reckoning
vpon fome receipt: but they
are beheld , vvith the light
of the illuminated vnder-
ftanding , as if vvith one
glaunce of an Ey , vve
should fee the excellent pi-
&ure of a rare maifter, vvith
admiration allmoft infenfi-
ble. So Saint Tiburtius faw
Paradice , when he walked
vpon burning Coales. So ,
all the Saints beheld beatitude when they amidft fo
many afflictions and tor-
ments ftood immoueable,
R 2   oppr.i-

oppreſſing the dolours and paines of body by the inondation of the minds contentment. From thence we neceſſarily meete with the fowrth Gate, which is a moſt ardent loue of things eternall : For as well Saint Thomas hath ſaid, the ſight of a temporall bewty cauſeth a temporall loue, ofttimes filling the ſoule with fire and flames : ſo the contemplation of Eternity createth eternall loue, which is a feruēt affection towards God, and all which belongeth to his Glory, as was that Mary Magdalen, who ſayth in Origen, that heauen, and the Angells were

a

a trouble to her and that she
could not liue, if she saw
not him who made both
heauen and the Angells;
she had passed seas armed
with monsters and tem-
pest, hauing no other sai-
les but her desires to meete
with her beloued: she had
flowne through flames, had
a thousand times grappled
with launces and swords
to cast her-selfe at his feete.
It is an admirable Alchimy,
for when one is arriued at
this perfect loue of God,
it turneth Iron into gold,
ignominyes into Crownes,
and all sufferings into delights.

At

At the fift Gate, which is called, the Reuelation of things eternall, God speaketh at the eare of the heart, and replenisheth a soule with goodly lights, and knowledges, euen then darting vpon it (as saith Gerson) certaine lightning-flashes of Paradice, as a Tortch reflecting rayes through the Crannyes, of a doore, or vvindovv; so (saith he) our Lady vvas enlightned in this life vvith liuely apprehensions of Beatitude which shottforth before her eies, like-flying fires.

And as the Knovvledges of our vnderstanding are nothing vvithout the feruors

uors of our vvill, vve from
this gate paſſe along to the
ſixth, vvhich is called the
Antipaſt of *Experience*; by
vvhich vve early begin to
taſt in this life the ioyes of
Heauen, and contentments
vvhich cannot be vnfolded.
A hundred thouſand ton-
gues may talkè to you of
the ſvveetneſſe of honey,
yet neuer ſhall you haue
ſuch a knovvledge of it, as
in taſting it: So a vvorld
ſtuffed vvith bookes may
tell you vvonders of the
ſciences of God, but neuer
ſhall you exactly vnderſtãd
it, but by the taſt of Experience. True ſcience (ſaith
S. Thomas vpon the Can-

R 4   ticles

ticles) is more in rellish then Knovvledge *In sapore*, then *sapere*. I had rather haue the feeling vvhich a simple soule may haue of God, then all the definitions of Philosophers.

Lastly the seauenth gate of Eternity is called *Operation Deifying*, or *Diuinized*, vvhich S. Denis termeth θεοδἶ. It is vvhen a soule vvorketh all its actions by eternall principles in imitation of the incarnate Word, and a perfect vnion vvith God. S. Clemens Alexandrinus calleth him, vvho is arriued at this degree Θεὸν ἐν ϭαρκὶ περι πολοῦντα, a litle God, vvho converseth in

mortall

mortall flesh : and addeth,
that as all good Orators
much desire to be like De-
mosthenes, so our principall
mistery in this vvorld is to
procure vnto our selues the
resemblance of God. It is
that vvhere in all our perfection consisteth.

---

*Of Perfection, and in what
it consisteth.*

SECTION III.

NOw, to the end this do-
ctrine, vvhich is some-
vvhat too sublime, may not
dalze your sight, and not
enkindle your courage , I
vvill deliuer a more familiar
Theo-

Theology, to wit, that there
are two sortes of perfection,
the one of glory, the other
of Pilgrimage: That, of glory is reserued for the other
life, and that of Pilgrimage,
is at this present our principall affaire. It is ordinarily
diuided into perfection of
State, and perfection of merit. Perfection of state, is
that of the Ecclesiasti-
call order of prelates of magistrates, and specially of re-
ligions, who are obliged by
the duty of their profession,
not onely to ordinary vertues, but to other more eminent. Perfection of merit
is that, which consisteth in
good manners. Trouble not
your

your felfe about perfection
of ftate , but liue conten-
ted in the condition wherein the Prouidence of God
hath ranked you, holding
it for a matter vndoubted,
that the greateft Philofophy in the world is well
to performe your office;
It importeth not vpon what
ftuffe you worke , fo you
worke well , for it is the
manner , not the matter
which fhall gaine eftimatiō.
Great dignities are oft-times great maskes vnder
which there is no braine;
and meane fortunes may
with fmall noyce perfor-
me actions of infinite value
with God.

Apply

Apply your felfe coura-
gioufly to perfection of merit, which refteth in the re-
gular gouernment of the
heart, the tongue, & hands
in perfect charity, Addict
your felfe to the practife of
fingular and folid vertues,
which on earth beget all
wonders, and in heauen pur-
chafe all Crownes.

The learned and deuout
Abbot Blofius did excellen-
tly well, when be abbreuia-
ted all fpirituall life vnto
twelue Maximes, which I
befeech you read, and often
compare with your Actions.

I.

In all you thinke fpeake,
and treate purely feeke the
honour

honour of God by the waies
of a sincere intention, and
endeuor aboue all to pre-
serue cleanesse and liberty
of heart.

II.

Submit your selfe with an
entire confidence of heart
to the maine streame of the
diuine Prouidence, in such
sort that you may find a soueraigne consolation in the
will and pleasure of God.
And whither you be in the
darkenesse of aduersity, whither you be enlightned vvith
the lightes of Prosperity,
vvhither your heart be
straightned by Tribulation,
or dilatetd by comforts,
vvhither you be ritch, or
vvhither

whither you be poore, euer
haue a perfect feeling of
the diuine Bounty. Take all
afflictions, and acerbityes
from the hands of his pater-
nall Piety, humbly, patiently, and (if it be possible)
gladly, holding it for certaine, that he either permit-
teth or ordaines all for our
good, and therefore onely
desire his will may be fullfilled now and for euer.

III.

Leaue the things to Gods
dispose, which you cannot
remedy, whither in your
selfe, or in an other, expecting with a long and meeke
patience, till he otherwise
ordaine it.

If

IIII.

If you can not beare an
iniury with ioy, at leaſt take
it with patience , turning
your ey towards God, who
was afflicted for you , and
who will haue you to be afflicted for him , and not the
man who perſecuteth you.

V.

Deſire rather to performe
the will of another, then
your owne, and be not too
obſtinate in your owne opinions , nor thinke any thing
comparable to holy obe-
dience.

VI.

Preſume not vpon your
ſelfe, diſpiſe none , account
your ſelfe the moſt vn-
woithy

vvorthy of all, & if any one
of your inferiors giue you
any counsell, courteously
receiue it, euer choosing rather to correct your errors,
then excuse them.

VII.

Affect Humility as much
as vvorldlings do honour,
that you may the better be
conformed to Chrift Iesus,
and his holy Mother.

VIII.

Seek not to please any one
out of vanity, and feare not
to displease by vertue: Desire
not to be knovvne, or beloued by any ouer familiarly,
especially by women, vvhose
very vertue are not alvvayes
loued vvithout daunger.

Iudge

IX.

Iudge not the facts and wordes of other rashly : Involue not your selfe in cares and superfluous busynesses, aboue all preserue your selfe from slaunder both of tongue, and eare.

X.

Be courteous and affable to all the world , taking compassion vpon the afflictions of your neighbour , and reioycing at his good successe. Euery where loue the Image of God, and hate none be they neuer so vnpleasing:if you must reprehend any one , do it with sweetnesse , and not with a turbulent indignation.

XI.

Despise the vanities of thé world, and the delights of the Flesh, which of their owne nature are very despicable;preserue your immortall spirit for a God eternall, and in his heart fixe all your comforts, and contentmēts.

XII.

Learne to satisfy your selfe with litle, in things which concerne the seruice of your body, remembring the pouerty which God, in whom all the treasure of ritches, and glory are, vnderwent for vs.

Many persons of quality disposing and excercising themselues vpon these precepts repts , haue come to the height of all vertues necessary for a spirituall life.

———— —— ————

Of vertues and their degrees.

SECTION IIII.

IF you desire to know their names, their properties , and degrees obserue the wise wordes of Plato, who saith there are fower sortes of vertues The First are Purgatiue; the second Illuminatiue; the third ciuill; the fowrth Exemplar. Purgatiue, serue to discharge our hearts from vices , and imperfections, ordinary to depraued nature; Illuminatine, establish the soule in a serenity, which resulteth from a victory gayned ouer passions; Ciuill, accommodate man to the duty he oweth to his neighbour; euery one according to his degree, and to a good conuersation amongst men; Exemplar, are those, which make the geatest progression into perfection, and may be considered as modells, from whece others who behold them, are to draw forth a Coppy.

Handle the matter so that your vertues may arriue to such a degree , that they not onely

onely may purge your heart
illuminate your soule, difpofe you to good conuerfation, but ferue others allfo
for a light to manifeft you
in them, by the imitation
of your good examples. I
briefly allfo add the definitions, and Acts of vertue,
by vvhich you may direct
your actions.

Of Prudence.

Prudence (according to
Ariftotle) is a vertue, vvhich
ordereth, and accommoda-
teth all things that concerne
the direction of our life.
Richardus de fancto Victore af-
figneth it fiue partes; to wit
S 3   Iudg-

Iudgment deliberation, difpoſition, diſcretion, moderation: Iudgement, diſcerneth good frō euill. Deliberation, ſheweth how to do all aduiſedly. Diſpoſition, teacheth the order muſt be obſerued. diſcretion, diſcouereth, how wee muſt ſometimes giue way to occaſions, and yield to humane infirmities, not peremptorily ſticking vpon ſingularity of opinions: Moderation, holdeth the ballāce and meaſure of each affaire.

The effects thereof (according to Albertus magnus) are, To proceed to the knowledge of God by the knowledge or ones ſelfe. To obſerue what is beſt in euery thing, and to embrace it:

To way the beginnings,
progreſſions , and yſſues of
affaires ; To order your
thoughts that they go not
out of God; your affections
that they be not too much
employed vpon creatures;
your intentions , that they be
without mixture, your iudgments, to diuert them from
euill , and apply them to
good; your wordes,to poliſh
them; your actions,to weigh
them;all the motions of your
body , ſquarely to guide
them. To gard your ſelfe
from fower rockes , which
diſturbe all affaires, to vvit,
Paſſion , Precipitation , vanity , ſelfe-opinion , ſingu-
larly to eſteeme this ſecret;
S 4   To

To know, to elect , to execute.

Of Deuotion.

Deuotion is a promptnesse
of the mind to things, which
appertaine to the seruice of
God, the parts whereof are,
Adoration , Thankfgiuing ,
Oblation, Pennance, Praier,
Mortification , Vnion with
God by contemplation, Fre-
quentation of Sacraments,
Conformity of will to the
diuine Prouidence , & zeale
of foules.

Of Humility.

Humility (according to S.
Bernard) is a vertue, which
causeth

causeth a man to disesteeme himselfe out of a profound knowledge he hath of himselfe. The principall pointes thereof are, well to vnderstand ones selfe; litle to prize ones selfe; To fly from humane praise; To preserue the heart free from the itch of renowne; Generously to despise worldly things; To loue a retyred life; To protest, and freely confesse your faultes; To hearken willingly to counsell; To yeild to others; To submit your will, and iudgment to obedience; To auoyd splendor, and pomp in matters which cōcerne vs; To conuerse gladly with the poore.

Of

Of Pouerty.

Pouerty, is the moderatrix of couetousnesse, which regardeth temporall things; the parts thereof are to cut off superfluities; To haue no inordinate care ouer worldly things; To beare patiently the wants of necessary things; To entertaine a perfect nakednesse of spirit.

Of Obedience.

Obedience (according to Saint Bonauenture) is a reasonable sacrifice of your owne will, and (according to Saint Iohn Climachus) a life without curiosity, a

volun-

voluntary. death , a confident hafard. The pointes thereof are, to execute what is commanded , readily, manfully, humbly , indefatigably , allthough it be contrary to your owne inclination. To make an entire refignation of your own iudgment, opinion and will; when you are commaundingly fent vpon harfh, and difficult . employments ; to hafte with alacrity vfing no delay, excufe, or reply ; To be indifferent for all things; To defire nought, nor refufe any thing ; To appoint your felfe nothing , nor prefume any thing ; To be more ready for humble and painfull

full things, then splendid,
and lesse burthensome.

Of Chastity.

Chastity is a continence
from impure pleasures, the
partes whereof are : purity
of mind and body; Carefull
watch ouer the senses; Flight
from occasions; Honesty of
speach; mortification from
curiosity; Exact behauiour;
Heed ouer ones selfe.

Of Modesty.

Modesty is a composed-
nesse of your selfe, which
consisteth in the gouern-
ment of the whole body,
gesture, attire, sport, recreation, and aboue all of the
Ton-

Tongue , wherein is to be
repreſſed Detraction, Con-
tention, Boaſtes, diſcouery
of ſecrets, Idleneſſe, Importunity , Irreuerence , and
falſe Silence.

Of Abſtinence.

Abſtinence, is a vertue,
which moderateth the con-
cupiſcence that relateth to
the delectation of ſenſe.
The partes thereof are; To
haue no other rule , then
neceſſity , in all which concerneth the pleaſures of
body ; To feare the leaſt
ſtaines of ſuch things , as
raiſon iudgeth diſhoneſt,
and to perſeuer in all holy
ſhame-

shamefastnesse ; To obserue
the Fastes commanded, and
to add some out of deuo-
tion ; To banish all curiosity
of dyet, of apparell, & sensuall pleasures.

Of Fortitude.

Fortitude , is a vertue,
which confirmeth vs against
pusillanimity that may hin-
der good actions. It hath
two armes, whereof the one
is to vndertake, the other to
suffer. Aristotle assigneth it
fower partes , which are ,
Confidence, Patience, Loue
of labour, and Valour.

Of Patience.

Patience, is an honest suf-
ferance

ferance of euills incident to
nature, the parts thereof are;
To suffer couragiously the
losse of goods, sicknesse, sor-
rowes, iniuries, and other
accidents: neither to complaine, nor grone, but to
hide your euills with discretion; To be afflicted in innocency for Iustice; Yea sometimes by good men; To
desire, and embrace perse-
cutions through a generous
desires to be conformable to
the patience of the Sauiour
of the world.

Of Iustice.

Iustice is a vertue, which
giueth to euery one what
apper-

appertaineth to him, and all the Acts thereof are concluded in this sentence; measure another by the measure you desire for your selfe.

Of Magnanimity.

Magnanimity (according to S. Thomas) is a vertue which inclineth to great things by the direct wayes of Reason. The Acts thereof are to frame to your selfe an honest confidence by purity of heart, and manners; To expose your selfe reasonably to things difficult, and terrible, for the honour of God; To be neither charmed with prosperity, nor deiected by aduersity;

sity; not to shrinke at obstacles. Not to rest vpon meane vertues. To despise complacencies, and menaces, for the loue of vertue; To honour God alone, and for his loue to make no esteeme at all of fraile, and perishable things; To preserue your self from presumption, which many times ruineth great spirits, vnder pretext of Magnanimity.

Of Gratitude.

Gratitude is the acknowledgment, and recompence of benifits receiued, as much as we can. The Acts thereof are to retaine the memory

T   of

of a benefit, to professe, and publish it, To render the like, without further hope of reciprocall good turnes.

Of Amity.

Amity is mutuall good, well grownded vpon vertue, and community of fauors; The Acts there of are; To choose frends by reason, for vertues sake; communication of secrets, consent of will; life seruiceable, and ready for good offices; Protection in aduersities; obseruation of integrity in all things; care of spirituall profit accompanyed with neces-

necessary aduise in all loue,
and reuerence.

Of Simplicity.

Simplicity is nothing els,
then the vnion of the interior man with the exterior.
The Acts thereof are; To be
free from disguize; neuer to
ly ; To faigne, nor Coun-
terfect; not to presume, To
auoyd equiuocations , and
doublenesse of speach ; To
interpret all you see in the
best sense; To handle affaires with sincerity; to auoyd
multiplicity of employ-
ments , and vndertakings.

Of Perseuerance.

Perseuerāce, is a cōstancy in

good workes to the end, out of an affection to persist in goodnesse, and vertue. The Acts thereof are; stability in good, repose in our functiōs, offices, and ordinary employments; Constancy in good entreprises; Flight from inouations; To walke with God; To fixe your thoughts, & desires on him; Neither to giue way to acerbityes, nor sweetnesse, which may diuert you from good purposes.

Faith.

Faith is a Theologicall vertue, by which we firmely belieue all the misteryes vvhich are reuealled vnto vs by the authority of God, who

who reuealeth them vnto vs.

1. Its Acts are, Submiffion of Iudgmēt to Gods Church which is the Interpreter of his Trueths.

2. To fly, and deteſt all in-nouatiōs, which are not ag-greable to the belieſſe of our Fore-fathers, and to the lawes ordained vs by ſacred Councells.

3. To auoyd the compa-ny of Hereticks; and though one be bownd to loue the perſons, yet neuer to loue their errors.

4. To profeſſe your faith freely without bluſhing, and to defend it (if need be) with the hazard of all account moſt pretious.

T 3   *Hope.*

Hope.

Hope, is a Theologicall vertūe, by which we hope true cōforts, grounded vpon the power, and Goodneſſe of God.

1. The Acts thereof are, cō-tempt of humane Hopes, the more freely to enlarge your heart to diuine.

2. An antipaſt of eternall bleſſings, which we begin to taſt in thought during the pilgrimage of this life.

3. An enquiry into the ſup-ports, which may fomēt our hopes, as are the merits of Ieſus Chriſt, the protection of our Lady, the aſſiſtance of Angells, and the interceſ-ſion of Saintes.

4. A

4. A firme confidence in the Goodnesse of God, in aduersities & temptations, which Crosse vs.

Of Charity towards God, and our neighbour.

CHarity, the true Queen of vertues, consisteth in the loue of God, and our neighbour; The loue of God appeareth much in the zeale we haue of his glory; The acts thereof, are; to embrace abiect & painfull things, so that they aduaucethe saluation of our neighbour; To offer vnto God for him the cares of your mind, the prayers of your heart, and the mortification of your flesh; To make no accep-

T 4   tion

tion of persons in the excercize of charges ; To let your
vertue be exemplar.

To giue what you haue, &
what you are for the good of
soules, and the glory of God;
To beare patiently the dif-
commodityes , and difftur-
bances which happen in the
performance of your duty;
Not to be difcouraged with
the fucceffes of improfpe-
rous endeuors; To pray feruently for the faluation of
soules;ro affift them both in
matters fpirituall and temporall , according to your
power;To roote out vice,&
plant vertue and good manners in all ; who depend on
you.

Of

Of Charity in conuersation.

Charity in ordinary life consisteth in taking in good part the opinions, wordes, & actions of our Equalls; To slaunder no man, nor despise any; To honour euery one according to his degree; To become affable to all the world; to be helpefull; To suffer with the afflicted; To take parte in the good successes of those, who are in prosperity; To cary the heart of others in your bosome; To haue more good deedes then specious complements; To employ your selfe diligently in the workes of mercy.

The

The degrees of euery Vertue.

THe deuout S. Bonauenture deciphereth vnto vs certaine degrees of vertue, very confiderable for practife, the names of which you may heere partly fee.

It is a high degree in the vertue of religion perpetually to extirpate fome imperfection, & much higher alfo daily to encreafe in vertue, and moft eminent to be infatiable in matter of good workes, & neuer to thinke to haue done any thing.

In the vertue of Trueth, it is a high degree to be true in all your wordes, & much higher

higher allſo to defend trueth
couragiouſly, and moſt ſu-
preme to defend it with the
preiudice of thoſe things,
which are deareſt vnto you
in the world.

In the vertue of Prudence,
it is a high degree to know
God by his creatures; and
much higher allſo to know
him by the Scriptures, but
moſt high to contemplate
him by the ey of Faith.

It is a high degree to know
your ſelfe well, and much
higher to gouerne your
ſelfe well, and much higher
to take a good ayme in all
your affaires, but a moſt
high degree aptly to mānage
the ſaluation of your ſoule.

In

In the vertue of Humility, it is a high degree freely to confesse your faultes, a much higher degree to bow amidst Greatnesse, as a Tree surcharged with fruit; but a most high degree couragiously to seeke out Humiliations, and abasements, so to become conforme to the life of our Sauiour.

It is a high degree (as saith an auncient Axiome) to despise the world, and much higher to despise no man; but more high to despise ones selfe, and most high to despise despight. In these fower wordes you haue the whole latitude of Humility.

In

In pouerty , it is a high degree to forsake Temporall goods, & much higher to forsake sensuall amities, but most high to make a diuorse from your selfe.

In chastity, it is a high degree, to bridle the tongue . much higher to guard all the senses, more high purity of body, higher yet cleanesse of heart, and much higher an alienation from worldly amities, but highest of all to banish pride, and Anger , which haue some affinitie with Impurity.

In Obedience , it is a high degree to obey the law of God , and much higher to submit ones selfe

to

to the Commaunds of a
Man, for the honour you
beare to the Soueraigne
Maitter, but more high to
submit your selfe with an
entire resignation of opinion, iudgment: affection,
will, and most high to obey
in difficult matters, gladly,
couragiously, and con-
stantly, euen to death.

In patience, it is a high
degree, to suffer willingly
in your estate, in your Kinred, in your good name, in
your person, for expiation
of your sinnes & more high
to tolerate the asperities of
an enemy, or of an vngra-
tefull man, you being inocent, and much higher to
                        endure

endure much , and com-
plaine of nothing , but moſt
high to beare croſſes and
afflictions , and to embrace
them as liueries of Ieſus
Chriſt.

In mercy , it is a high degree to giue temporall thĩgs
much higher to pardon in-
iuries, moſt high to oblige
thoſe , who perſecute vs. It
is a high degree to take pitty
vpon the afflictions of body,
and more high to be zealous
for ſoules , and moſt high
notably to cõpaſſionate the
torments of our Sauiour in
the memory of his paſſion.

In the vertue of Forti-
tude , it is a high degree
to conquer the word , much
higher

higher to fubdue the flefh,
moft high to ouercome ones
felfe.

In temperance , it is a
high degree well to order
your eating, drinking, flee-
ping, watching, game, re-
creation, your tongue, wordes, and all the geftures of
your body , a much higher
degree well to gouerne affections, and moft high
throughly to purify your
thoughts , and imagina-
tions.

In Iuftice, it is a high
degree to giue vnto your
neighbour what belongeth
to him; a much higher to obferue reafon with your felfe,
and moft high to offer
vp

vp to God all the satisfaction which is due to him.

In the vertue of Faith, it is a high degree to be well instructed in all we should belieue, and much higher to belieue it simply, and religiously, and more high also to professe it by your good workes, and most high to côfirme it by losse of goods and life, when need is.

In the vertue of Hope, it is a high degree to haue good apprehensions of the power of God, much higher to entrust all your affaires to his diuine Prouidence, & higher yet to pray vnto him, and to serue him with feruor and purity without in-

V   termis-

termiſſion, and moſt high
to hope in him, in the moſt
deſperate and forlorne occaſions.

Laſtly for the vertue of
charity, which is the accō-
pliſhment of all the reſt,
you muſt know, it is of
three ſortes. The firſt is charity beginning, The ſecond
charity more confirmed, &
the third is perfect Charity.

Charity beginning hath
fiue degrees 1 Diſlike of paſſed crimes. 2. A good purpoſe of amendment. 3. A
Reliſh of the word of God.
4. Promptneſſe in good
workes. 5. Compaſſion in
an others hurt, and ioy at
his good happ.

Cha-

Charity more confir
med hath fiue other de
grees, The 1. a great pu
rity of conscience, purged
by a very frequent Exa-
men. The 2. lessening of
concupiscence. 3. A vigo-
rous excercise of the in-
ward Man: For as the good
operatiós of exterior senses
are signes of the health of
body: So the holy employ-
ments of the vnderstan-
ding, the memory, the
will, are tokens of a spirituall life. 4. A ready obseruation of the law of
God. 5. A tastful know-
ledge of celestiall verities,
and maximes.

Perfect Charity likewise
recko-

reckoneth vp fiue other degrees. 1. To loue ones enemies. 2. To take aduersities
cōtentedly, & couragioufly.
3. To haue no humane ref-
pects, but to meafure all
things by the feare of God.
4. To be free from the affection of creatures. 5. To
hazard your felfe for the
faluatiō of your neighbour.

There are allfo added
nine other degrees of fera-
phicall Loue, which are fo-
litude, filence, fufpenfion,
infeperability, infatiability,
indefatigability, rapture, lā-
guor, extafy, which would
require a long difcourfe,
but it is from the purpofe
of my prefent intention.

Fower.

*Fower orders of such as aspire
to perfection.*

SECTION V.

COnfider at this time
what vertues, and in
what degree you would practife them : For there are
fovver fortes of people,
which afpire to perfection.

The firft are very inocent,
but nothing generous for
the excercife of vertues. The
fecond , befides inocency,
haue courage fufficient to
bufy themfelues in worthy
actions , but are very fpa-
ring

ring towards God, and do
meafure their perfections by
certaine limits which they
will not in any fort exceed:
wherein they are not vnlike
the Oxe of Sufis, who out
of a well drew his vfuall
number of buckets of water,
cheerefully; but do what you
could, it was impoffible to
make him go beyond his
ordinary proportion. The
third order is of the feruent,
who are innocent, generous,
and vertuous, without re-
ftriction, but they will not
take charge of others, thinking themfelues troubled
enough, with their owne
bodyes, wherein they may
many times be deceyued.

The

The fowrth order comprehédeth thofe, who being enabled through much induftry, do charitably open themfelues to the neceffities of their neighbour, when their helpe is called on, thinking it is to be in fome fort euill, not to be good, but for ones felfe.

Obferue what God requires of you, and be you an emulator of the moft aboundant Graces: But if the multiplicity of thefe degrees of vertue trouble you, I will fhew you a way of perfeétion much fhorter, and more eafy.

*A short way of Perfection prac-
tised by the Auncients.*

SECTION VI.

THe auncients had this
custome to reduce all
vertues to certaine heads,
and some addicted themselues with so much feruor &
perfection to the excercise
of one sole vertue, that pos-
sessing it in a supreme degree with one single linke
they insensibly drew a long
the whole chayne of great
actions. One studied all his
life time the gouernment
of the Tongue, another
Absti-

Abſtinence, another meek-
neſſe, & another obedience.
So, it was fownd at the
death of a holy man na-
med Or (as ſaith Pelagius)
that he had neuer told a
ly, neuer ſworne an oath,
neuer ſlaundered, neuer ſpo-
ken but vpon neceſſity : So
Phaſius (as writeth Caſſian)
ſayd vpon his death-bed,
that the Sun had neuer ſeene
him take his refection : for
he euery day faſted, till the
Sun was ſett. So, Iohn the
Abbot witneſſeth, that the
Sun had neuer ſeene him in
anger, that he neuer had
done his owne will, nor
had at any time taught o-
thers, that, which he had
noſ

not first practised himselfe.
There was need of much
strength of spirit to come
to this. If you desire matters
more imitable be yee assured you will lead a good
life, disposing your selfe
perpetually to the practise
of these three things : *To
abstaine, to suffer, to go forward in well doing*, as saith
Saint Luke in the Acts of
the Sonne of God. *To ab-
staine.* 1 By abstaining from
all vnlawfull things, and
sometimes euen from law-
full pleasures, out of vertue.
2. By mortifying concupiscence, anger, desire of estimation, and ritches. 3. By
gouerning your senses, your
will,

will, your Iudgment, and
continually getting fome
victory ouer your felfe, by
the maiftery of your paf-
fions. *To fuffer* 1. By endu-
ring the burthens of life
with great patience, accoun-
ting your felf happy to participate in the paines of our
Sauiour; which are the moft
noble enfignes of your Chri-
ftianity. 2. By endeauouring
to vfe a fingular meeknefe
in bearing with the contradictions, & defects of others.
3. By vndertaking fome au-
fterities of body, with counfell. 4. By holding a firme
footing in Goodnefe, all-
ready begun. For as fayd
old Marcus the Hermite:
The

The wolfe and the sheepe neuer aggree together, to breed vp their yong: so labour, and loathing neuer make vp perfect vertue. *To go forward in well doing*, By becomming diligent, and obliging towards all the world, euery one according to his degree: but aboue all, haue still before your eyes, the list of the workes of mercy, as well spirituall, as temporall, as a lesson whereon you are to be seriously examined, eyther for life, or death eternall. And for this purpose some Saints had for all Bookes these wordes in their Library.

To

To vifit.
To quench
 thirſt.
To feed.
ro redeeme.
To cloath.
To lodge.
To bury.

To teach.
To coũſell.
To correct.
To cõfort.
To pardon.
To ſuffer.
To pray for
 the dead.

The beſt Art of Man, is to oblige another. The time will come when death will diſarray vs euen to the bones, and leaue vs nothing, but what we haue giuen to God.

Meanes

Meanes to become perfect.

SECTION VII.

FOR this purpose you
must be perpetually
watchfull ouer your actiõs,
& be like a Seraphin sprin-
kled all ouer with eyes, and
lightes, as Bessarion said.
You shall know your pro-
gression in vertue, when
purged from great sinnes,
you begin to apprehend
the least, when you shall
feele your selfe free from
ardent desires of interest,
and honour, when you
shall haue discharged your
tongue

tongue from flaunder, and
vanity, when your heart becommeth very much puri-
fyed in its affections, and
that you draw nearer to In-
differency. The meanes to
make your felfe perfect in
this manner, is, Firſt to be
enflamed with a feruent defire of perfection. Secondly not to neglect the extir-
pation euen of the leaſt imperfections. Thirdly, to
haue a good director, who
may be vnto you, as the
Angell Raphaell was to
young Toby, and confe-
quently to conferre often
with fpirituall men, and to
be enflamed by their Ex-
ample. Fourthly to make

a

a Poasy of flowers of the
liues of Saintes, that you
may take into you the
odour, and imitation of
them. Fiftly to render your
selfe constant in good purposes, and to offer them
vp to God, as by the hands
of our Lady, and your An-
gell Guardian.

How

*How one ought to gouerne him-
selfe against Temptations,
Tribulations & Obstacles
which occurre in the
way of vertue.*

SECTION VIII.

IN fine seing in the practise of vertues, you must
still haue armes in hand, to
destroy the powers of your
aduersary, and to aduaunce
the affaires of saluation, recall to your memory the
Twelue Maximes, which I
proposed against those obstacles, which may happen.

X   The

The way to refift tempta-
tion is not to frame within
your felfe a fpirituall infen-
fibility, which is moued at
nothing. It is hard to attaine it, fo fenfible is felfe-
loue, and had you it, it were
to be a ftone, not a man. It
is not to driue away one
temptation by another, and
to do one euill to be freed
from another; for to purfue
fuch a courfe, is, like waf-
hing ones felfe with inke.
It is not to hide one from
all accidents that may fall
out, and neuer to do good
for feare you muft fight
againft euill, but to refift
couragioufly, in that manner as I will fhew you; That
great

great man Iohn Picus of
Mirandula hath collected
twelue notable Maximes,
the practife of which is
moft profitable to enable
you for fpirituall Combat.
1. Maxime. That you muft
be tempted on what fide
foeuer it happen: It is our
profeffion, our Trade, and
our continuall exercife. The
Eagle complayneth not of
her winges, nor the nigh-
tingale of her fong, nor
the peacock of her Trayne,
becaufe it is their kind; & it
is as naturall for man to be
tempted, as for a Bird to
fly, to fing, to prune her
feathers. If you forfake the
way of fpirituall life, fea-

ring to be tempted; and
turne towards worldly contentments, hold it for an
infallible trueth you shall
there by become the more
engaged in them, and which
is worse, without comfort,
without honour, merit, or
reward: you shall cast from
you a paper-crosse, which
if you well knew how to
mannage it, it would, burthen you no more, then
feathers do the Bird: you
shall tast it off (say I) to
take vp another, hard, vn-
easy, and bloudy, and which
will make you become a
companion with the bad
thieffe. The great Prelate
Sidonius Apollinaris relateth

teth that a certaine man called Maximus being arri-
ued at the height of honour
by vnlawfull and indirect
wayes, was much troubled
from the very first day, and
breathing out many sighes,
spake these wordes *O Da-
mocles* I esteeme thee most
happy to haue beene a King
onely the space of a dinner
time : It is now a whole
day that I am such, and
I can no longer endure
it.

2.   Maxime. Remember,
that in the affaires of the
world, we long combat,
we trauell painfully, and
reape fruitlesslly. The end
of one toyle is the begin-

X 3   ning

ning of another, nor in
our paines-taking haue we
any other hope but perpe-
tually to labour, and a
temporall toyle drawes
after it an eternity of
paine.

3. Maxime. Is it not a
meerefolly to belieue a Paradice, a life euerlasting,
a Iesus Christ, who made
a ladder of the Crosse, to
afcend to the throne of his
glory, and you meane while
to be desirous to liue
heere with armes a crosse?
To fee the maister open
the way of Heauen through
fo many thornes, and the
feruants to be loth to tread
on any things but flowers?

To

To see vnder a head all wasted and worne with sufferings, a delicate member, as one should put feete of flaxe to a brazen Colossus.

4. Maxime. Were there no other fruit in Tribulation, but the conformity which we there by haue with Iesus Christ, the soueraigne wisdome, that would be a high reward. A braue Captaine said to a soldier, who dyed with him: Thou who wouldst haue beene vnknowne all thy life time, it is no small honour for thee to dy to day with thy maister. And who would not account it for

X 4   a

a great glory to haue the
sonne of God for Captaine,
for companion, for spe-
ctator, for Theater, for
guerdon in all his affli-
ctions, and tribulations?
Who would not esteeme it
a great dignity to be daily
crucified with him? To
stretch forth his armes, and
handes vpon the Crosse, by
with-holding them from
violencyes, from rapines,
concussions, into which
the spirit of lying transpor-
teth vs? To fetter your feete,
by hindering them to runne
after the vnbridelled desires of your heart? To make
bitter your Tongue by sub-
duing the pleasures of tast?
To

To couer your body all ouer
with woundes by suppres-
sing the incitements of flesh,
by a holy mortification? To
lessen your selfe by the contempt of honour, according
to his example, who being
able perpetually to walke
on the winges of Cheru-
bins, would creepe amongst
vs like a litle worme of the
Earth? what a braue thing
it were to say, that, which
S. Paule did; *I beare the
markes of my Sauiour Iesus on
my body.*

5. Maxime. Not to con-
fide in humane remedies,
when you vndertake to o-
uercome a temptation; It is
not a thing which wholy
depen=

depēdeth on vs, It is fit God
go before, and that we readily there to contribute our
free will. For if he watch not
ouer vs, it will be hard for
vs to keepe centinell. No
creature is so weake, as he
who accounteth himselfe
strong. Many good things
are done in man, which man
doth not. And man doth not
any good, which God doth
not, (sayeth the Councell
of Orange). Who thinkes
to resist temptations with
out his helpe, is like him
who hastneth to the warres,
and stumbleth at the thres-
hold of the doore. And therefore an affectuall meanes
in this battell is to be very
diligent

diligent in prayer, especially
at the first entrance of a temptation.

6.   Maxime. When you
haue vanquished a tempta-
tion, take good heed, you
do not presently lay downe
armes and become remisse,
as if you had no other enemy
to fight withall. As Distrust
is the mother of safety, so
ouer much security is the
gate of daunger. If your
enemy perpetually roame
vp and downe like a roring
Lyon, become you on the
other side a watchfull lyon
in the centinells of the God
of Hoastes.

7.   Maxime. Content not
your selfe onely not to be
beaten

beaten but affaile your enemy. When Sathan layes a
fnare for you, make you it
an inftrument of merit. If
he prefent you a good
worke which glittereth in
the world, thereby to tempt
you with pride, do the good
worke and leaue vanity, re-
ferring, and applying all to
the greater honour of God.
8. Maxime. When you are
in combat fight couragioufly, as if you were allready
certayne of victory. Turne
away the ey of your confideration from what you
fuffer, and hold it perpetually fixt vpon the reward.
A great vnhappyneffe which
maketh many to fall head-
long

long into Temptation, is,
that they haue their mind
so bent vpon the thought
of the trouble, that they
cannot haue time to reflect
on the reward, which wai-
teth on them. When the
forty Martyrs were in the
frozen Lake, thirty nine
of them had their ey on
the future Crowne, which
they expected, and one of
them thought vpon no-
thing but his Torment, All
of them remayned victo-
rious, except this wretched
creature, who loosing the
glory of patience, came out
of the lake, to dy presently
after in Infidellity. Do you
not imagine, that that
which

which comforted our Sauiour on the Croſſe, in the bottomleſſe Abiſſe of Calumnyes, and dolours, was a mirror of Glory, wherein he beheld all his paſſions crowned? See what you are to do: ſtay litle on the preſent, and reſt in a ſtrong apprehenſion of the future, & euer haue theſe wordes of S. Paule in your heart. *A moment of Tribulation, produceth in vs an eternall weight of Glory.* Fight then brauelly as if it were the leaſt temptation which ſhould aſſaile you and be you aſſured that heerein reſtes the prooffe of your predeſtination. When you haue ouercome it, gouerue

uerne your selfe like one
who is ready preſt to reenter into the liſt and make
one victory the ſteps to another.

9. Maxime. Though you
be valiant, braue not Temptation, by caſting your ſelfe
into the occaſions thereof,
thorough preſumption of
heart: He who much affec-
teth hazard, in ſtead of finding glory, ſhall trace out
his owne tombe.

10.   Maxime. A Souerai-
gne meanes, to conquer temptations, is ſeaſonably to
diſcouer the countenances
of them, freely to open your
heart to your ghoſtly father
to declare your thoughts,
well

well to vnderstand them, to
confider their nature, and
to fee the power they haue
ouer your foule. That ordinarily happeneth, which
the good Epictetus, faith.
It is not the thing that trou-
bleth, vs, it is our fantafy.
How many temptations
would be ouercome by
flighting them, if one tooke
but a litle leifure to laugh at
them? we make Elephâts of
flyes, and in the confufion
of our fcattered thoughts,
we apprehend dwarfes
as if they were gyants: we
are like litle children, who
for feare of a vizard hide
themfelues crying in their
nourices bofomes: but take
away

away the vizard , and giue it
them to handle , and they
will make sport with it.
How many thinges, seeme
terrible and impossible to vs
which we find ridiculous,
and easy to ouercome, if we
put but a finger to them!
In temptations of pusillanimity it is good to represent
to your selfe the false Gyants, as Dwarfes:but in that
of Concupiscence, you must
not despise any thing, rather
feare litle threads , as if they
would become huge cables.
Both in the one and the
other there is nothing to be
done, but to dash these litle
Babylonians against the sto-
nes withstand beginnings,

and suffer not your enemyes to fortify themselues to your preiudice.

11. Maxime. The stone of offence and scandall to many is, that they liuely represent to themselues the sweetnesse of sinne, but neuer consider the glory deriued from the victory ouer a sinne. As soone as Man is plunged in the puddle thereof, behold a blushing soule, drenched in pensiuenesse, melancholy, and despaire, whom a lothsome pleasure, which hath passed away as a dreame, furnisheth from a dreame with a huge heape of scornes, sorowes and confusions: whereas on the contrary he who

who hath refifted, finds
himfelfe content, gene-
rous, aduaunced and fatis-
fied with holy comforts,
which come from the pa-
radife of God. Few men
reuolue this thought, which
S. Cyprian fo much recom-
mendeth:which is the caufe
why the number of the damned is fo great, and yet doth
it not feeme to you a matter
very reafonable, that a man,
who a thoufand times hath
yeilded, once in his life time
try the fweetneffe that is in
the victory ouer a temptation, to reioyce for euer?
many haue beene diuerted
from a great, and manifeft
precipice, by confidering
Y 2   thefe

these wordes. Well! go to!
*To yeild to sinne, what will be
the end of its. So dearely to pur-
chasse repentance? To render vp
a renowne of so many yeares, as
a prey to a most vnhappy moment of pleasure? Where is the
faith promised to God? Let vs
at least seeke out some place
where he is not; and where is
he not? So many starres, so
many Intelligencyes, wherewith the world is replenished,
are as many eyes of God to behold thee; He himselfe looketh
into the bottome of thy conscience. Aske leaue of him if thou
will sinne. But how will you
aske it, and how will you obtayne it? Excercise a litle patience, and this temptation will
vanish*

vanish away, as a clowd. Thou
goest about to commit a sinne,
the pardon whereof is very vn-
certaine, but it is doubtlesse
throughout all eternity (when
thou hast committed it) God
himselfe cannot make it to be
vndone.

12. Maxime. Thinke not
you are the lesse acceptable
to God, when he suffereth
you to be tempted, yea with
dishonest temptatiõs, which
to chast soules are extremely yrkesome, Alas why! If S.
Paule, that Cherubim scort-
ched with celestiall ardors,
who fixed his foote vpon
the front of starres (if we
follow the opinion of S.
Ambrose, Thophylact, and

Y 3　　Oecu-

Oecumenius) felt the ſtings
of concupiſcence in a fleſh
rapt to the third heauen,
thinke you, you hauing
ſome good diſpoſitions to
do well, you needs muſt be
freed from the warres of nature, which perpetually
keepe in the liſts of humility, your mind a litle too in-
dulgent to it ſelfe.

Finally follow the Coun-
ſell of Caſſian, daily conſider the paſſions which
grow in your heart, as a
fiſher man beholds the fiſh
ſwimming in the water,
of purpoſe to catch them.
Looſe end vpon that which is
moſt predominant in your
heart, from what roote it
riſeth

rifeth, when it began, what
progreſſion it hath made,
what empire it ordinarily
vſurpeth on your ſoule,
what effects it produceth,
whither it be ſenſuall, or
ſpirituall, what vſeth to fo-
ment it, what remedies haue
moſt ſerued to diuert it.
Prouide meanes and coun-
ſell to extirpate it proceed
therein with courage and
feruour as in the acquiſi-
tion of an incomparable
good.

But obſerue there are
ſome are tempted with a
feare to be tempted, and
who are paſſionate (ſaith
Tertullian) for feare to become paſſionate, who are

distracted out of the apprehension of distractions, which they too troublesomely reiect. Sleight temptations must be driuen away by contempt, Great by a' good renuntiation, and if they often and violently disturbe vs', and that we cannot so readily apply remedy therevnto, let vs take it as a spirituall Martirdome.

Remedies

Remedies againſt Paſſions, &
Temptations , which
proceed from euery
vice.

SECTION IX.

Firſt. To conſider that
Paſſion is a motion of
the ſenſuall appetite , which
proceedeth from the Ima-
gination of Good or Ill,
with ſome alteration of
the Body.

2. That there are eleauen
Paſſions, ſix in the appetite
of Concupiſcence, which
are Loue , Hatred , Deſire,
Auerſion, Ioy, Sadneſſe.

Fiue

Fiue in the appetite of Anger, Hope, Despaire, Boldnesse, Feare, Wrath. That there are two wayes to ouercome all Passions, the first whereof is a precaution of mind against all occasions, and vaine apparencyes of all worldly things, & the second a serious employment on better things, as Prayer, study, labour, and affaires: but aboue all you must aske of God the light, and strength of his holy Grace, which infinitely surpasseth all humane remedies.

Let vs now add some preseruatiues against Passions, and the most ordinary vices.

Against

Against carnall loue.

Carnall loue is an inordinate inclination to the impure pleasures of Flesh, which is accompanyed with blindnesse of heart , with Precipitation, Inconsideration, Inconstancy , Hatred of God (because he forbiddeth euill bodily pleasure) with an exorbitant affection of this present life, and with the despaire of life euerlasting.

1. Against this vice we must consider the barrennesse of wordly loues, which are the true gardens of Adonis, where nothing is to be gathered

thered, but petty flowers en-
uironed with many thornes.
2. To set an estimate on
things, and not to be deceyued with semblances.
3. To guard your senses, to
fly the opportunityes, and
occasions of sinne, & aboue
all to haue a particular re-
course to God, vpon the
first impression of thoughts.
4. To pull your selfe by
maine strength from the presence of obiects, and to diuert your selfe by serious
thoughts, and good employments.
5. Often to set before your
selfe the imperfection, the
Ingratitude, the liuety, the
Inconstancy, the treachery
of

of creatures, which we most
seruilely affect.

*Against Auersion, Hatred
and Enuy.*

Enuy is a discontent at
anothers good which is accompanyed with Hatred,
sadnesse, ill Ioy, slaunder, In-
uentions, and cunning practises to hurt another, If you
desire to resist it.

1. Esteeme nothing great
in this world ; This is the
way not to enuy at all.

2. Loue onely the great
enheritance of the land of
the liuing , which is neuer
lessened by the multitude,
and store of those who pos-
                    sesse

sesse it.

3. Consider attentiuely the motiues, which stirre vs vp to the loue of our neighbour, as the participation of one same nature, same life, same bloud, same profession, and so many other reasons, which are as many knottes of amity.

4. The wretched life of Cain one must lead in the envy, anxiety, vnquiet, and rage of a distempered mind, which causeth the Immortallity of its Essence, to contribute to the Immortality of its punishments.

5. To see how Enuy e're it is aware oft times serues for the exaltation of such

as

as are enuyed.

Against desire, Hope, and worldly Ioy.

Desire, is a loue of a good absent ; Hope , a motion of the Appetite , which pur-fueth the knowledge one hath of a good future, pos-sible , and some what diffi-cult; Ioy, a contentment of the mind in the fruition of a good. Against these pas-sions when they are irregu-lar, you must represent to your selfe.

1. The disturbance of a pi-ning spirit. 2. The insatia-tiability of desires.

3 The combats and bat-tayles which must often be waged

waged to fatisfy one fole
defire. 4. The difhonour of
refufall , infupportable to
a generous foule. 5. The
dependance , and feruitude
which muft be vndergone to
be acceptable to thofe,
from whom we expect the
accomplifhment of our wifi-
hes. 6. The facility we haue
in offending God by ouer
much greedyneffe of tem-
porall thinges. 7. The wretched , and fleeting pleafure
we take in things the moft
ardently defired.

8. That God often permit-
teth vs the accomplifhment
of our defires for punifh-
ment of our imperfections.

Againſt

Against Sadnesse and De-
spaire.

Sadnesse is a paine of the
minds for some euill hap-
pened. Despaire, an absence
of a good impossible , or
which we iudge to be such.
There is a holy Sadnesse, as
is that we conceyue for the
passion of our Sauiour , or
for our sinnes, which is a
guift of God , and not a
grieffe.

There is a furious one,
which hath no eares , and
which is rather cured by
miracles, then precepts.

There is one naturall
which comes from humor

Z   and

and another vicious, which
is fed by ill habits, and neglect of ones owne saluation.

1. Against this we must
consider that our desires &
loues oft times cause our
Sadnesses: and that the true
meanes to lessen the cares
which deuoure vs, is to
sweeten the sharpe, and ardent affections we haue
towards worldly things.

2. The litle account we
make of God is the cause we
often trouble our selues for
friuolous things, eyther
such as threaten vs, or such
as are happened. He who
would throughly loue our
great God, who deserueth

to

to poffeffe all the loue of heauen and earth, would haue no further feare, nor become fad, but for the loffe of God, whom no man loofeth, vnleffe he purpofely forfake him.

3. There are none but the teares of the damned which are remedy-leffe one who may yet be in the way of heauen fhould not vndertake the condition of a litle Hell, and he who can hope this great All, ought not be contriftated with any thing.

Againft euill Boldneffe.

Euill Boldneffe is an vndertaking prefumption,

against which we must thinke.

1. That to behold in euill things, is to haue a deadly instrument of your own vnhappinesse, which mokes all the exorbitancies of your heart to breake forth, to render them the more punishable.

2. That there is no assured boldnesse against the power of God, who in the twinkling of an ey ouerthroweth the sonnes of Titan, to speake with the scripture.

3. That the strongest things are destroyd by the wakest. Lyons haue beene deuoured by flyes, and wretched rust

ruſt , conſumeth the hardeſt
of mettalls.

4. That to be bold out of
the preſumption of ſtrégth,
is the way to become ridiculous in your enterpriſes,
and vnfortunate in your
ſucceſſes. You muſt not
ſoare to the ſun with the
winges of a Batt, nor ſayle
ouer the Ocean in the ſhell
of a Tortoyſe.

Againſt Feare.

Feare is an apprehenſion
of euill to come , which you
ſhall vanquiſh with theſe
conſiderations.

1. Neyther to deſire , nor
loue any thing inordinately,
Z 3   This

This is a paſſage to Tranquility , where vnto Feare
neuer arriueth.

2. To haue a ſtrong cha-
rity towards God , and to
loue him feruently , not
doubting to be reciprocally
beloued by him. This is the
way to enter into a ſtrong
confidence : For what euill
can we feare againſt vs,
when God is for vs.

3. Wee many times feare
euills , which are the ſources of great bleſſings ſome
are not really euills , other
are much leſſe then we
make them , other will neuer happen. Why will you
put your ſelfe into a priſon where you are not , or
on

on the rack by your meere
imagination ? 4. He who is
resolued to suffer all which
God will, takes an able remedy against all sortes of
feare : For he that is Maifter of sorow, swayeth ouer
Feare, since the euill present
is more yrksome then the
future.

5. There are naturall Ti-
midityes, which are extremely tyed to flesh, vnlesse
we vanquish them, and
sweeten them by acqua-
inting our selues with the
things we feare and by
conuersation with per-
fons confident and coura-
gious.

Z 4   Against

Against Anger.

Anger, is a motion which proceedeth from the opinion of contempt: against which we must consider.

1. That it depriueth vs of six things very precious, to wit, of wisdome, ot iustice, of Ciuility, of Concord, of Trueth, and of the spledor of the spirit of God.

2. That it sodainly transfigureth a man into a litle Monster. 3. That it is preiudiciall to health, which we so tenderly loue.

4. Besides that, it much vilifyeth the person, who is surprized with it, and especially if he be in any emi-

nen-

nency of life, or dignity.

5. That its effects are cruell deuastations pernicions, successes shamefull, and falls most often irreparable.

6. The contentment we haue to haue kept back an ill word, which might haue marred a good businesse.

7. Alienation from curiosity and incenesse, cutteth the sinewes of anger assunder. The lesse we are curious, the more we are humble; and the more we are humble, the lesse we resent the offence of things, which are with out vs.

8. We must preuent occasions, & not giue ouer much power in our heart, to all

those

those things , the losse of which may trouble vs.

9. To eschew accidents of place, persons, recreations, and of affaires , which vse to trouble the peace of our mind.

10. If you find your selfe inwardly moued, to bridle the tongue, that the ressentments of the heart appeare not outwardly, to reenter into your selfe , and to aske truce of your passion, constantly belieuing , that we shall pardon many offences, if we begin but to vnderstand before we grow angry.

Against Vanity and Pride.

Pride

Pride is an irregular appetite of proper excellency, which confisteth in fower principall things, which are; To afcribe the good you do wholy to your felfe , & that it is due to your merits; To prefume of your felfe , To attribute that to your felfe, which is not in you, To defpife others , with defire to be, and to feeme fingular.

1. Againft this paffion it is good to often fet before your eies the notable vanity of all worldly things.

2. The mifery of our prefent condition , wherein all things inuite vs to Humility.

3. The vanity of opinion, which hath nothing in it

but

but wind.

4. The Blindnesse, incapacity, Inconstancy, and perversnesse of the iudgments of men, who many times loue, and admire all that, which is the most vicious.

5. The frailty of honour, and reputation sought by vnlawfull wayes.

6. The Torments and tortures of a vayne spirit.

7. Inflation in good successes, and faintnesse in bad.

8. The surprizall of your sleights, and weaknesses, which cannot be hidden from the most iudicious.

9. The worme which gnaweth all good workes by the meanes of vanity, and shame-

shamefull depriuation of
eternall blessings, to labour
in the search of terrestriall
smokes.

Against Gloutony.

Gloutony is an inordinate
appetite of meate, & drinke,
if you desire to ouercome it.
1. Represent to your selfe
the miserable state of a spirit
brutish, and be myred in
flesh. 2. The hardnesse of
heart. 3. The stupidity of
vnderstanding. 4. The in-
firmityes of body. 5. The
losse of Goods. 6. The ruine
of reputation. 7. What a
horror it is to make the
members of an vncleane
crea-

creature of the members of
Iesus Christ. 8. What an
indignity it is to adore, and
serue the belley, as a brutish
and base God: 9. The great
invndation of sinnes which
proceed from this source.
10. The punishements of
God vpon the voluptuous.

Against liberty of Tongue.

Liberty of Tongue is an
itch to speake without li-
mit, against which we must
consider that it is the throne
of vainglory.
2. An vndoubted note of
Ignorance. 3. The gate of
slaunder. 4. The fore runner
of Floutes. 5. The Architect
of

of lying.

6. The defolation of the
fpirit of piety. 7. The dif-
fipation of the cuftody ouer
the heart. 8. The infepe-
rable companyon of Idle-
neffe, as witneffeth S. Iohn
Climachus.

Againſt Sloth.

Sloth is a remiffneffe of
fpirit in vertuous actions,
which is accompanyed with
an effeminate foftneffe, with
a dullneffe, with an ouer
much loue of life, with an
apprehenfion of labour, &
of all things vneafy to flefh.
Againft which we moft
weigh. 1. The indefatiga-
ble

ble toyle of all creatures in the naturall & ciuill world. 2. The facility of good workes, since Grace was giuen by Iesus Christ. 3. The anxiety of a spirit wandring, and floating. 4. The shame, and contempt. 5. The confusion at the day of iudgment. 6. The losse of irreconerable time.

Against Auarice.

Auarice is an excessiue desire of gaine which is waited on by hardnesse of heart, Disturbance, Violence, Deceit, Periury, & Treason. It bereaueth the mind of the hope of heauenly things, It
fixeth

fixeth it to the Earth, maketh it odious to others,
infupportable to it felfe,
and many times drencheth
it in the laſt of miſeries.

Aa

THE

THE THIRD
PART OF THE
DIVRNALL.

Affaires , and their importance.

SECTION I.

THE third employmént of the day, is in the affaires we handle, whether it be for the publique, or for your particular in the gouernment of your family, or in discharge of some office.

fice. A good emploiement is
a good deuotion, and there
is nothing more to be feared
then Idleneſſe , which is the
very ſource of ſinne. He who
laboureth (ſayd the aun-
cient Fathers of the deſart)
is tempted but vvith one diuell; he vvho is idle hath
them all at once. No man is
ſo noble, vvho ought not to
find out ſome manner of
employment. Had Iron vn-
derſtanding , it vvould ſay,
it had rather be vſed in frequent labour, then to grovv
ruſty in the corner of a
houſe.

*Two heads, to which affaires
are reduced*

SECTION II.

VVE must in affaires
consider the *Sub-
stance* and the *Forme.* The
Substance ; for it is a great
vvisdome to make a good
choyce in this point , to vndertake good emploiments,
to leaue the bad , which do
nothing but trouble the
mind , and choke the sense
of deuotion , especially
vvhen there is no obligation
to vndertake them. Those
are truely ill in health vvho
out

out of curiosity interpose
themselues, to knovv, to
do, and to sollicite the affaires of others : It is enough
(sayth the Emperour Anto-
nin) for euery one in this
life to do that vvell, vvhich
he professeth. The Sun doth
not the office of the rayne,
nor rayne of the Sun. Is it
not a meere frenzy, To see
men in the vvorld, vvho
haue nought to do, but to
meedle vvith all, and performe nothing.

As for *forme* in the excercise of charges, of offices,
and affaires, therein must
be vsed *Science*, *Conscience*,
Industry, & *Diligence*. *Science*
1. In learning that vvhich

Aa 3   is

is profitable to be knovvne,
for difcharge of your duty.
2. In informing yourfelfe of
that from others vvhich you
cannot vnderftand by your
felfe 3. In giuing eare moft
gladly to aduife, by exami-
ning, and pondering it vvith
prudence, and in all things
directing your felfe by counfell. *Confciēce* In performing
all vvith good intentions,
and great integrity according to lavves both diuine,
and humane. *Induftry*, In
doing all things difcreetely,
peaceably, vvith more fruit
then noyce : in fuch fort
that no anxiety may appeare
in employments, like vnto
that Prince, of vvhom an
Auncient

Auncient faid, That in his moft ferious affaires, he feemed allvvaies at leyfure. *Diligence*, In carefully fpying out occafions, and doing euery thing intime , and place, vvithout *diforder , confufion , Paſſion, Haſt, Irreſolution,* and *Precipitation.* Thefe are the defects vvhich for the moft part deftroy good order. He, vvho hath neuer ſo litle vnderftanding , and good difpofition fhall euer find vvherein to bufy himfelfe, (efpecially in vvorkes of mercy)amongſt ſo many obiects of the miferyes of ones neighbour.

A a 4 Of

Of the Gouernment of a Family.

SECTION III.

HE hath fomevvhat to do, vvho hath a family to gouerne. A good Father vvho breedeth his children vvell, that they may one day ferue the common vvealth performeth an importāt bufyneffe for the publique. A mother vvho traineth vp a litle Samuel for the feruice of the Tabernacle, as did S. Monica her fonne Augu-ftine, obligeth all pofterity. A maifter, and a miftreffe, vvho

vvho keepe their domesti-
que seruants in good order,
merit much before God,
and men. Fovver things very
considerable are to be vsed
therein, *Choyce*, *Gouernmēnt*,
Example , *Entertainment*.
Choyce in the consideration
of the Quantity, Quality,
Capacity, Fidelity of those
vvhom you take into your
seruice. As for Quantity, it
ought to be proportionable
to your estate , and reue-
nevves: It is a folly to make
ostent of a number of seruants for meere vanity : As
did Herod the sophister (according to the relation of
Philostratus,) vvho allovv-
ed his sonne tvventy, fovver
pages

pages, euery one of vvhich
bare the name of a letter of
the Alphabet: for so blockish
was this child, that he could
not othervvise learne the
first elements. The starres,
which are least in compasse,
are nearest the pole, and
men least embroyled in affaires, many times most approach vnto God. A huge
pompe of followers, is an
argument of much scarcity:
were there such a Beast,
as the Hebrew Fables fai-
gned, to whom we should
daily giue the grasse of a
thousand Hills, for his
share, would you account
him more happy, then
the litle nightingale, which
is

is satisfyed with a few seeds,
or the Bee which liueth on
dew? The Ritch man hath
need of many Crownes, the
poore of a litle bread; both
are indigent, yet the one
lesse then the other, since he
hath lesse need. A great
traine of seruants makes not
a man the more happy: For
there is not any one a greater Maister, nor better o-
beyed, then he, who well
knoweth how to serue him-
selfe.

For Quality: Take good
heed least you resemble Sor-
cerers, who will not stick to
fee the diuell, so they may
make vse of his seruice for
their purposes. Either you
must

must take good seruants, or
make them such; In the one
case there is good happ, and
in the other very often much
difficulty : For many are not
vnlike S. *Vincent Ferrerius*
his Asse , who did more for
a Carter who called vpon
the diuell, then for his Maister who lead him a long a
Gods name; which the holy
man seing, he ridd himselfe
of him , not being able to
endure such brutishnesse
euen in a Beast : and can you
imagine, that for the necessity of your affaires, it would
be fit for you to beare with
a man who hath neither
God, nor conscience : that
so your children may there
by

by at first suck in the ve-
nome of his conuersation.

For Capacity; It is most
certaine, that besides Honesty, there must be ability
in charges : and allthough
it be said that Saintes are
good for euery thing, yet
God doth not allwayes giue
them both the desire, and
the meanes to deale in all
manner of professions. Our
abilityes are limited, as are
our mindes, and euery one
hath his particular talent,
which ought to be vnder-
stood by such as will make
vse of it.

For fidelity; It is one of
the Qualityes, which the
Ghospell attributeth to a
good

good feruant : You haue
reafon to require it , and
prudently to obferue it, not
by fufpitions, and iealou-
fies, which ferue to no other
vfe, but to vexe thofe who
haue a difpofition to do
well. A man many times is
made faithfull , and loyall
by being thought fo , and
diuers by perpetually fea-
ring to be deceyued , haue
taught others to deceyue,
fhewing them the ready
way to finne by their di-
ftruft, as (fayth the Romane
Philofopher,) you muft afford your officers the command , and liberty , which
their places require , and
not euery hower reprehend
them

them for trifles : Howſoe-
uer you muſt carefully re-
ſerue the maine ſtate of your
owne affaires to your owne
knowledge : For it is as
great a folly indifferently to
truſt all men , as to be diffi-
dent of all the world.

---

*Of Gouernment in ſpirituall
things.*

SECTION IV.

WHen you haue hap-
pened vpon a good
choyſe , Gouernment is no
difficult matter : For S. Au-
guſtine ſayth , there is nothing

thing so easy as to persvvade good amõg those who much desire to put it in execution. Gouerne your family in that manner, as the good S. Elzear did his, of vvhich the reuerent Father Biner hath framed so natiue a pourtraict. First banish vice and scandall from your house. Let loue-daliances, and such vnvvorthy things neuer approach thither, no more then the serpent to the flovver of the vine: Let not surfet and Drunkenesse, nor loose ryot so much as know your gate: Let Game find no harbor there: Let neyther vncleane word, nor blasphemy be heard, because

as

as Nabuchodonozor cau-
fed the Pages which wai-
ted on him to learne his
language : So the diuell
teacheth thofe his Dialect,
who allready feeme to be
in his power.

Vice being exiled, accu-
ftome your houfhold peo-
ple to fome deuotion, cau-
fing them carefully to heare
Maffe, efpecially on Fe-
ftiualls commanded, cal-
ling vpon them to frequent
the Sacraments according
to their condition, and af-
fembling them as Saint
Charles Borromeus did in
the euening, or at fome
hower of the day, to fay
fome

some prayers together, if conueniency of place permit : as allso to see how they are instructed in the articles of Faith.

Your example will do more, then all your wordes : For the life of a good Maister and Mistresse is a perpetuall Censure in his house. Those who seeke to gaine their good opinion, desire to be like them and by that meanes whilst they endeauour to be esteemed, they become good. We liue in an Age, wherein we stand more in need of Examples then precepts. Seruants cleaue

to

to the pillars of a houfe,
as Iuy to great Trees and
in a vvord at the Com-
mand of Great ones all
Wills are of vvaxe, fo
flexible they are. It is fit
likevvife (to make good
this opinion) that you be
liberall according to your
meanes in the entertain-
ment of your family by
honourably difpofing of
requifite expences , both
in matter of neceffity, &
Decorum. For netts are v-
fed to catch fifh , and li-
berality as golden threads
to catch men.

Befides , forget not in
the maine mannage of your
affai-

affaires to inuoke moſt particularly the aſſiſtance of
God, oft-times ſaying ouer
theſe wordes of Salomon
in the Booke of Wiſdome.

*My God, giue me the wiſ-
dome, which waiteth on thy
Throne, ſend it from the Sanctuary of Heauen, and the
ſeate of thy Maieſty, that it
may abide with me, trauell with
me, and may make me to know
thy bleſſed will, to put it in
execution.*

Preſerue your ſelfe from
indiſcreete haſt in the beginning of a buſyneſſe, from
anxiety in the progreſſion,
and deſpaire in the end. If
your

your proieſt proceed well,
giue prayſe to God , and
example of modeſty to your
neighbour. But if matters
ſucceed not to the Tone
of your owne. liking, practiſe to follow the meaſure
of the diuine Prouidence,
which maketh all the Har-
monies of the world : The
ordering of a buſineſſe is in
your power , not the e-
uent. You muſt not wiſh
all matters may happen, as
you would but take them
as they happen. Accuſtome
your ſelfe not to be con-
triſtated at wo.ldly accidents, no more then you
would be at an ill dreame.
Bb 3   For

For all heere beneath paſ-
ſeth away as a dreame: and
we do much , if looſing
all we retayne this belieffe,
but by a long ſoothing of
our proper wills, we haue
allmoſt forſaken (as ſaith
Caſſian)the ſhadow of Pa-
tience.

Aduiſe

Aduise for such as are in employments, and Gouernments.

SECTION V.

SAint Bonauenture wrot an excellent Treatise, which he calleth the winges of the Seraphim, where in he giueth most sage instructions to those, who are in office and gouernment, where of heere in part, take the substance, and marow, which I intreate you throughly to tast. He giueth his Seraphim six winges, the first is, The zeale of the honor of God, which you ſhall attaine to by obſeruing fower things, To wit.

1. Neyther to commit, nor giue to thoſe who are vnder you the leaſt ſuſpition of euill, or ſinne.

2. Not to permit it in anv kind, not withſtanding the allurements which may ſoth you vpon one ſide, and the importunityes which will aſſaile you on the o-ther.

3. Neuer to be willing that an euill Act be done before it come to your knowledge, for that were to betray your conſcience.

4. To correct, and take
away

away diforders as much as you can poſſible. The ſecond wing which you ought to haue, is the *Spirit of compaſſion to* helpe the ſick, the aged, the feeble, the fainthearted, the afflicted, for they are poore Porcupines laden with prickles, and acerbityes, to whom you may be a ſanctuary, and a Rock of Refuge.

The third wing is *Patience.* In ſo many trauells, & cares, which are allmoſt inſeperable from charges, and gouernments. Patience in the ill ſucceſſe of affaires, which dò not allwayes proſper anſwerable to our endeuour, and good deſires.

Patience

Patience to tolerate the
vngratefull, who many
times throw ftones at thofe
who giue them hony-com-
bes, not much vnlike the
Atlantes, that fhot arrowes
againft the fun. Patience
in the occafion of wordes,
and affaires, when one
treateth with fuch people,
as are quickly difpleafed,
and heated with anger. °It
is a great vertue to mollify
them with a fweetneffe,
peacefull, filent and cha-
ritable, and as it were to
caft oyle into an enraged,
tempeftuous fea. An Aun-
cient, fayd, That he who
could well endure an in-
iury was worthy of an
Empire

Empire. His silence alone
will disarme a passionate
man , and prostrate him
at his feete , who seemes
lowdly to thunder ouer his
head.

The fowrth wing is
Example , which is especially obserued in three
things. 1. In putting into
practise the good Coun-
sells, and precepts, which
we teach others by word.
2. In mannaging dignity
and command in a man-
ner neither harsh, haughty,
nor arrogant , but sweet
affable , and communica-
tiue. 3. In entertayning
allso a decent and mo-
derate

derate grauity, that the character may not be vilifyed, which God impresseth on those, whom he calleth to charges, and commands.

The fift, and principall wing is called *Discretion*, without which all vertues become vices : For the honor of great Actions consisteth not so much in doing good, as in doing good, wel.

This Discretion is manifested in fower things, In mannaging good with good iudgment, In correcting euill; In well administring, and dispatching temporall affaires, recommended to your charge, and amidst these

these encombrances, to support, and preserue your selfe
as fresh water in the salt sea.

The mannage of good is
obserued in three principall
Acts. The first is to cause
those, who are vnder you,
strictly to obserue things
necessary, and which cannot
be omitted without disor-
der, or scandall. The se-
cond, to winne, and sweet-
ly attract euery one according to his condition, his
capacity, and discretion, to
workes the most perfect,
wherein they haue no for-
mall obligation. The third
to dispose with a good Oeconomy charges, and bur-
thens according to the in-
clinations

clinations, and strength of those spirits you gouerne.

As for correction, eyther they are sleight faultes of persons well conditioned whom you are to correct (and those are to be handled with much sweetnesse) or they are couert vices of some maligne consciences, which you neither ought nor can discouer; Heere you must exercize much patience, Industry, and wisdome, to vn-neastle vice, and draw the winding serpent out of his caue, as by the hand of a Mid-wife, (as saith the scripture) : or they are publique sinnes of desperate people, who offend

fend without hope of amendment; to the infection of
very many, and heere it is
where you must fortify
your selfe with all your
power, to take away the
euill, and the euill-doers.

As concerning temporall
affaires, vse them in such
fort, as we haue fayd be-
fore, and take good heed
you entangle not your mind
in them, as a Fish in the net
depriuing, it of the liberty
of the children of God, to
serue the world.

Aboue all, euer looke
well to your selfe, as the
mayne and prime piece of
your gouernmēt, keep your
conscience

cõscience cleane, confident,
and peacefull speaking and
doing all things with great
circumspection, and neuer
despising their counsell, who
are able to aduise you.

Lastly your sixt wing is
Deuotion, which is diuided
into three sortes, the one
common, the other particular, the third continuall. The
common consisteth in exactly performing duties of
piety within the limits of
your profession, and to do
them by way of imitation
of that heauenly warr-fare,
which is perpetually employed in the prayses of
God, and by way of edification of those to whom you

ow

ow this good example. Particular deuotion obligeth
you to seeke a particular refuge in the Tabernacle, following the stepps of Moyses, according to the necessityes of your charge. Continuall deuotion tyeth you to a most feruent excercize of the presence of God, which you shall witnesse by hauing a desire to please him in euery place, in all occasions, and in all actions, and by dedicating to him all your workes before you begin them, and at the end of them to set the seale of thankesgiuing, due to his diuine Maiesty.

Imprint very deepe into

your heart the wordes of
S. Bernard, which are in
his firſt booke of Confideration, fift Chapter.

If you be a man of em-
ployment, and that all the
world haue a ſhare in you,
Take a part in your ſelfe,
as well as others. Fruſtrate
not your ſelfe of a good, ſo
iuſtly yours, and be you
none of thoſe, who trauell
inceſſantly, and neuer returne back againe to their
lodging.

THE

THE FOVRTH
PART OF THE
DIVRNALL.

Recreation, and necef-
fity thereof.

SECTION I.

FOR as much as con-
cerneth Recreation,
which is vfed in com-
pany, at repaft, in honeft
Game, in walkes, in good
conuerfation, it is neceffary
to diuert the mind and re-
Cc 2   paire

paire the forces. Caſſian in his 24. collation, chap. 21. tells, that a Huntſman haning on a time fownd S. Iohn Euangeliſt ſporting with a partridge, was amazed, how one, of ſo great repntation could entertaine himſelfe with ſo ſlender a recreation. The holy Saint ſeing this man had a Bow in his hand, asked him, why he did not allwayes cary it bent, and he anſwering it would weaken, and marre it, the Apoſtle replyed, ſo is it with the mind of man, which muſt be ſometimes vnbent that it may ſhoote the better.

Pleaſures

Pleasures of Tast.

SECTION II.

NOte, you muſt vnbend, not looſen the mind: Preſerue your ſelfe from theſe exceſſes, which make men now a dayes as glotonous in the eyes, as Belly. It is a ſtraunge vanity to affect the reputation of knowing, and diſtinguiſhing the taſt of dainty morcells, to ſet all your mind to ſerue that part of the body, which hath leaſt of the ſoule, and to cheriſh a renowne, which

Cc 3 engroſſeth

engroſſeth onely with the fumes of the Kitchin. Vſe not your belly as Caligula did his horſe ; For he allowed the attendance and pompe of a Prince to a beaſt, to whom nature allotted nothing but Oates and hay : yet you do the like, when you beſtow ſo much coſt and endeauor to pamper the moſt beſtiall part in you, which the diuine Prouidēce would haue to be very ſparingly nouriſhed. Thoſe great feaſtes, which begin with vanity, and are lenghtned out with ſo much ryot, perpetually conclude in folly, and very often in repentāce. Nought

els

els is gayned from the pleafures of the throte, but a
body the more crazy, a pri-
fon of flefh the ftraighter,
and a death more fpeedy.
Vnhappy are the banquets,
which the hunger of the
poore accufeth before God:
It is aboue fixteene Ages
ago, fince they burned the
tongue of the ritch Glou-
ton, buryed in Hell, of fo
many tunnes of delicious
wines there being not left
him one filly dropp, to re-
frefh him.

If you defire to know
what the Banquets of the
aūcient Chriftians wereof,
which fhould be the modell
of ours, the excellent Tertul-

Cc 4   lian

lian frameth a difcourfe thereof in his Apology. Our
feaftes (faith he) fhew in
the beginning by their name
what they are : They are
termed Charityes, becaufe
they are inftituted for the
comfort of the poore : Our
table reffembleth an Altar,
and our fupper a facrifice:
We regard not what it coft
vs : It is a gaine to fpend for
pietyes fake. Our table hath
nothing which fauoureth
of bafeneffe, fenfuallity, or
immodefty; we there feed
by meafure, we there drinke
according to the rules of
Purity, we eate as much as
is neceffary for thofe who
muft rife at midnight to offer

fer their prayers to God:
we there speake and con-
uerse, as in the presence of
God, with hands washed,
and candles lighted; euery
one repeateth what he
knowes of holy Scriptures,
and of his owne inuention,
to the honor of God: Prayer
concludeth the banquet, as
it began it. From the ta-
ble we go vnto the excer-
cize of modesty, and ver-
tue: you would say if you
saw vs, that it were not a
supper we tooke, but a
lesson of sanctity; Alas!
Compare the feasts of many
Christians to this, and you
may as well paralell the
tables

table of Centaures, to the
banquet of Angells.

Take your refection as
an almes from heauen, and
complaine as litle as you
can of your viands ill dres-
sed, shewing therein your
litle care of those things,
which concerne the Body.

—— — ——

Of Game.

SECTION III.

FRet not your selfe li-
kewise in those Games
of hazard, which haue in
them so much auarice, feruor, and flames. Should

a

a man committ no other
finne, but to be conuer-
fant a third part, or the
moity of his time with
Kings & Knaues of Cards,
being inuited to the fociety
of Angells, fhould he not
do ill? But befides that
this euill Game is the inuention of the Frend Za-
bulon, as Saint Cyprian
obferueth in the Treatife
he wrot, toutching this
fubiect; It is the Altar of
Fortune, detefted by the
Prophet; It is the fhopp of
deceit; The fchoole of Auarice; The apprentifhip of
blafphemy; The Skirmifh
of choler; where Amityes
become enraged Thefts,
vnpunifs

vnpunished, and sweet mur-
thers are committed , and
from whence one commonly
ly caryeth away nought, but
a Tempest in the mind , gall
in the heart , and wind in
the purse. Who can at the
day of Iudgment excuse one
that gameth his gold away
with a profuse hand , and
keepes back the wages of a
seruant , or the life of a
poore creature , that pineth,
and quaketh with cold at
his doores. The soldiers of
Pilate threw dice on the
garment of the sonne of
God, as on the Bloud which
dropped from his Body:
but they were Hangmen,
and miscreants : who would
not

not tremble at a Christian,
that among so many Images of the suffering of the
sonne of God, without any
regard of times, of God, or
men, playes away the
bloud, eyther of his domestiques, whom he neigleteth, or of the poore,
whom he dispoyleth ? Take
away these sollaces, which
are brought forth, as the
Salamander in the teares of
heauen.

Clemens Alexandrinus
in his booke called the Pedagogue, well discouereth
that these games of cards,
and Dice, and such like were
ill receyued into the primitiue Church: For he sheweth
that

that such pastimes are often
times, as a Bubling, or ouerflow of delights ill rectifyed, and an indigestion of
euill Idlenesse.

If we must needs Game,
to giue satisfaction to o-
thers, we ought (at least)
to take care, it be for some
good purpose, that it be
among our equalls, and
without passion, litle, and
moderate, and for the auayle
of the poore.

Before Game, practise
purity of intention; In
Game, Modesty, Alacrity,
and Fidelity; After Game,
Discretion, and Silence.

Of

Of Dauncing.

SECTION IIII.

FOr Daunces, Bals, and Song, that is true which is faid by the holy Bifhop, and excellent Author in his Introduction, that they are like mufhromes, the beft of which are worth nothing. Ryot, vanity, foolifh expence, maskes, good cheere, night, youth, loue, liberty, are as daun-gerous councellors of wifdome, as euill inftructers of modefty.

One

One may amidſt thoſe
be ſanctifyed by miracle,
but we daily ſee many loſt
by infirmity: If we be more
infirme, then miraculous,
we ought to ſeeke for that
ſafety in the flight from occaſions, which we cannot
find in the ſtrength of our
mind.

The fable tells, that the
Butterfly asked the Owle,
how he ſhould deale with
the Fire, that had ſinged
the tipps of her winges; &
he aduiſed her, not to come
neare, ſo much as to the
ſmoke thereof. With what
conſcience can a faithfull
ſoule frequent worldly recreations, which haue layd
ſo

so many blemishes vpon its purity. Must we stay till we be burnt before we go from the fire? I wonder at those, who would spiritualize Bale and reuellings, and accord them with frequent communioes; They would in conclusion fall vpon the Industry of the Emperour Adrian, who layd Adonis in the cribb of Iesus. There must be so many circumstances of intention, of time, place, persons, and manner to season such pleasures aright, that the absence from them would be much easyer, then the vse.

D d

Of

*Of wanton Songs, and
Comedies.*

SECTION V.

IF you fpeake of wanton
Songs, of the reading of
naughty bookes, of im-
modeſt Comedyes and
ſtage-playes, your conf-
cience (which is the ſcho-
ole Miſtreſſe of the ſoule)
whiſpers you more of
that, then perhaps you
are willing to belieue.
Such recreations ſerue as
Harbingers to diſorder,

as

as hands to Senfuallity, as
Tinder to finne, and fcan-
dall to vertue. Euill, at that
time entreth into you,
through all the Gates of the
Senfes, and iffueth not out
againe, but by the pofter-
ne of pennance, which is
not allwaies open to our
Indifpofitions. A yong
foule is furprized therein,
as in a golden fnare, and
verily to perfonate a finne,
is not onely to teach it, but
command it : For we liue
now in an Age, where to
know, and do ill, haue (as
it were) no Medium to fe-
perate them, and if we be
vertuous, it oftentimes
proceedeth rather out of
Dd 2   the

the Ignorance of vice, then from precepts of vertue, (sayth Saluianus.)

Of Pleasure in walking, and running.

SECTION VI.

REcreations the most innocent are euer the most commendable, as are those, which are taken in the Countrey in the exercise of Body : For the Countrey life (sayth worthy Columella) is the Cousin-german of Wisedome.

Take

Take away the comforts
which are had in Churches,
in matters of Iuftice, learning, Arts, and commerce,
what are great Cittyes, but
great prifons? Men liue there
as Birds in Cages, They
pefter one another, and be
dawbe each other by a frequent and contagious con-
verfation. The turmoyle of
affaires, the importunity
of vifits, the fottifh tyranny
of Complements deceyue
them of the moity of their
life. In the Countrey, the
Heauens, the Ayre, the
Earth, the waters, which
Cittyes depriue vs of, are
afforded vs wiht farre more
freedome. There, all gods
Crea-

Creatures speake to vs face
to face , and tell vs the
wonders of the Creator.

The Chriſtians of the primitiue Church made Her-
mitages of their Farmes, to
ſownd a retreate from af-
faires of the world , and to
hearken to the hower of
their laſt repoſe : but many
now a dayes make of their
Gardens Temples for Bel-
phegor , where , no other
Deityes are adored , but
the Belly , Riot , Game, and
Impurity.

Many vſe aire-takings, &
Barley breakes , where they
run not farre without ſtum-
bling : For they rather reſ-
ſemble the liſt of Atalanta,
and

and Hippomenes, then the
race wherin S. Paule ex-
horteth the Christians to
runne. There oft it is, where
the senses flattered with a
thousand delightfull ob-
iects, put themselues into
the field, where the bloud
is enflamed, the tongue is
vnlosened, concupiscence
enkindled, and where false
liberty many times teareth
off a piece of the scarfe,
which hitherto veyled the
face of Modesty, and auda-
ciously now becomes a Por-
tresse to wantonesse. Such
kind of sacriledges, dry
vp. Yeares, bring disorder
into seasons, sterility into
the bowells of the earth,

and despaire into our My-
seryes.

*Of fower conditions of Re-
creation.*

SECTION VII.

YOur Recreation ought
to haue fower remar-
keable things ; *Choyce Of
Persons, Good intention, Innocency, Moderation. Choyce of
persons*, by auoyding ill company, as the most daunge-
rous shelfe, of life : For the
Fellowship, and society of
badmen is like vn-do bund-
les

les of thornes, which keepe
together to burne and crac-
kle in the fire: Your amityes should be vertuous,
faithfull disintereſſed, if
you thence expect any fruit.
Good Intention: Such as is fit
to mainteyne health, and
ſtrength to ſerue the ſoule:
For a good man, ſhould
find merit in play, and Re-
paſt, as S. Frauncis, who
roſe in the night, and fed
before a poore hungry fryer,
to take from him the ſhame
he had to eate at an vnvſuall
hower.

Innocency, for conſideration muſt be vſed therein,
leaſt nature be diſſolued
into a brutiſh life, alltogether

ther vnworthy of a gene-
rous foule. Pack hence
Gloutony, retchleſſe game,
bold ſcoffing, and Detraction, which is now a-dayes
very hard to be auoided.

The moſt ordinary Booke
in companyes of men, is
man himſelfe : You ſhall
find very few who in this
Age delight to talke of the
new, or old Teſtament, nay
verily not ſo much as of
the auncient Roman Con-
ſulls, or Ægiptian Pyra-
mids, or of the antique
warres of Cæſars : Men
ſtudy the Booke of the Times, talke of Garbes, Ha-
bits, countenances, eſtates,
qualityes, affaires, cuſto-
                        mes

ines, and alliances: and allthough they haue no pur-
pofe to offend any, yet is
it a matter very eafy in fo
great a variety of difcourfe
to let many wordes fall,
which had beene better to
haue beene filenced. It is
a fingular induftry to make
a good difcourfe flide into
conuerfation, whither it be
vpon occafion, queftion,
confequence, narration, or
propofition, as the Reue-
rent Father Iaquinot obferueth in his Addreffe.

Moderation fince (as the
wife man faith) as we muft
not exceffiuely glut our
felues with honey : fo ought
we

we to take heed, that re-
creations which are made
to refreſh the mind, tend
not by exorbitancy to diſ-
ſolution : You muſt ob-
ſerue what Time place, and
perſons require , and to
find out your ſelfe in ſome
recreation , you muſt not
go out of your ſelfe by pro-
fuſion.

Of

Of vicious Conuersation, and firſt of the Impertinent.

SECTION VIII.

THe Hebrewes ſay, game Anger, Glaſſe, and Conuersation are the windowes of the ſoule, which many times let it ſee more then it would. That man is wiſe, who makes vſe of conuersation as of a file to polliſh his mind, and euer to render it the more apt for its functions.

Vicious conuersation, is drawne (as it were) to three

three heads, to wit, The
impertinent, the vaine, the
maligne, The impertinent,
as the clownish, the sottish,
the troublesome , which
happeneth to many through
the want of Prudence, Fashion, and Ciuility.

Theophrastus , one of
the quaintest witts of Antiquity, relateth some passages thereof, which he
saith he obserued in his
time, as arguments of the
weaknesse of mens iudgments. Some (saith he)
lay hold of one going vpon an important busynesse to communicate with
him (as they say) a matter of great weight , and
when

when it is told, it is fownd
to be a meere foppery. O-
thers entreate a Traueller,
who comes out of the coū-
trey, extremely weary, to
wealke with them. Others
hale a man out of a fhipp
vpon difankring; to entertaine him with follies on
the fhore. Others come to
beare witneffe, when the
fuit is determined, and puf-
fing, and blowing bring a
long with them the Phifi-
tian to fee one newly de-
ceafed. Others boaft they
know the way well, and
promife the reft to be their
guide; but prefently wan-
der and go aftray, and pro-
teft.

test they haue lost their aymes. Others most grossly are inquisitiue after busynesses, and aske a Generall of an Army whither he goes, and what his plot is. Such allso (saith he) are many times to be fownd so rusticall, that admiring nothing (which is worthy of admiration in a ciuill life) stick vpon the way to behold an Oxe, as men in a rapture, and in company haue no better manners, then to take their dogg by the muzzle, and say; *O what a braue dogg is this, how well he keepes the house.* Such conuersation is able to vilify a man, and to

take

take from him all the estimation, he might acquire in his profession.

------- --- --- -------

Of vaine Conuersation.

SECTION IX.

VAine conuersation is that of babblers, flatterers, vainglorious, and such like. This poore Theophrastus, fell (in my opinion) into the hands of a Tatler, seing he so well describeth a man, who with much passion proclaymed

E e the

the prayſes of his owne
wife , and then told all he
had dreamed the night be-
fore; Then, what he had to
dinner, then, that he had an
ill ſtomack: From thence taking his flight , he diſcour-
ſed of the times and aſſured
them that men of this Age
were much short of the
Auncients. Afterward he
ſaid corne was good cheape;
That there were many for-
raigners in the City; That
if it happened to rayne,
the yeare would be fruit-
full; That he had a field to
be ploughed; That Damip-
pus gaue the greateſt waxe-
light at an offering ; That
there vvere ſo many ſtai-

res

res in such a piece of buil-
ding; and that he had num-
bred them, and a thousand
such like things. Such people (added this Author)
are more to be feared then
a feauer. He who desireth
to liue at rest, should sel-
dome keepe them company.
Horace makes mention of
one very like, who put him
into a sweate that droppd
downe to his heeles, and
when he saw him so ve-
xed, that he knew not
which way to turne him. I
well see (Sir) saith he) *that
I trouble you :* but there is no
remedy, since I haue met
with you, it is but fit I
waite vpon you, for I thanke

God I haue nought els to do.

Flatterers are much more
acceptable , though they
are many times more daun-
gerous : For they will tell
you all the world casteth
an ey on you : That you
are much esteemed , & that
all the towne talkes of such
a busynesse that succeeded
well with you ; That you
haue an excellent wit, han-
some body , a good grace,
a dainty garbe ; That any
thing sitts well vpon you,
& that it seemes when Na-
ture had made you she brake
the mould, holding it impossible to create such another.
If you speake the enioine all
the world silence , then as
Oracles

Oracles they magnify your
wordes: and if you ieere any
one, they burſt themſelues
with laughter to pleaſe you,
& deify all your imperfections. This is the meere
poyſon of amities, and hoo-
dwinking of humane life.

The vainglorious will
ordinarily entertaine you
with their owne prayſes,
and will haue a thouſand
flight ſingularityes in their
cariage, in their apparell,
their ſpeach, their houſes,
their traine, to giue notice
thereby they haue ſome
what tranſcendent in them
aboue other men. The fore-
mentioned Author ſayth
he hath obſerued thoſe

who accounted it for a
great glory to haue a
Moore for a lackey the
more to be noted , and if
they facrified an Oxe , they
fet the hornes ouer their
gate to make the world
take notice of their Sacrifice ; and to conclude were
fo great louers of themfelues
that they made Epitaphs e-
uen of their dogges , fpe-
cifying their Age , their
Countrey , their qualityes,
and conditions. Thefe are
teftimonyes of a foule vaine
and void of all manner of
Humility.

Of

Of mischievous Conversation.

SECTION X.

Mischievous Conuersa-
tion is the worst of
all, as that of the harsh, who
render themselues vnsocia-
ble in Company; That, of
the contradictions, who
haue for their Motto, *Yea*,
and *No*, and are still vpon
oppositions, euen in True-
thes the most euident; That,
of the crafty, and guile full,
who seeke to discouer all
the secrets of others, whilst
they hide themselues vnder

a Maske of diſſimulation,
and in a perpetuall Laby-
rinth of wordes, faigning
to be ignorant of all they
know, to know wath they
know not, to forget a pro-
miſe, To pretend to wiſh
them well, whom they
would deceyue, and many
ſuch like things: That, of
the prowd who contemne,
and diſdaine all what themſelues are not; That of the
chollerique, who are diſ-
pleaſed vpon euery occa-
ſion; That of ſcoffers, Buf-
fons, and ſlaunderers, who
are obſcene, bitter, and of-
fenſiue in all occaſions.

It would be a tedious bu-
ſyneſſe for any man to exa-
mine

mine all this particularly,
and I fhould be glad to haue
vnfolded all this in a Treatife of manners , and paffions , wherein I would
hope to giue my Reader
contentment , were it not
that the deffigne of this litle
Booke diuerted me.

It would be litle to the
purpofe , to make fo long
a piece of it, and much better it is to conclude well,
them enlarge ill.

The

*The Condition of good
Conuersation.*

SECTION XI.

LET me in few wordes
tell you , that S. Ber-
nard, S. Thomas and other
learned men are of opinion,
that in conuersation you
should be affable, and frendly , yet not ouer familiar,
nor too curious in other
mens matters, not suspitious,
light, litigious, disconten-
ted , affected , magistrall,
captious , exceptious , no
scoffer, no anxious one, no
Dotard

Dotard; not churlish, cere-
monious, nor talkatiue; not
too plyant, & eafy, not chollerique, iealous, prowd, nor
vaine, as thofe who through
vanity (which is onely ritch
in fooleries) perpetually
idolatrize themfelues, as a
Deity : But one muft cary
himfelfe with great difcretion and modefty; he fhould
fport without debafing,
laugh without burfting, take
recreation without effemi-
nacy, be conftant without
obftinacy, prudent without
craft, fimple without ftu-
pidity; often he muft dif-
femble ill, ftill aduaunce
good, correct his owne
faultes

faultes by thofe which are difpleafing in others, euer to beare away from the garden of Graces fome fruit into his houfe , and if any fecret be there learned (which were fit to be concealed) to make of your heart a fepulcher for it.

You fhall find there are ordinarily fiue qualities, which render conuerfation frendly. The firft is an obliging fafhion , which fweetly foweth good turnes, whence in time , and place , we behold recompences to arife. This defire to do good to all the world is a hooke we muft continual-

tinually keepe in the wa-
ter ; For men thereby are
more aduantagiously ta-
ken, then fishes; and such
there haue beene, who sea-
sonably giuing a glasse of
water , haue gayneth the
prime places in a King-
dome, as we know by the
history of *Thaumastus* , and
King *Agrippa*.

The second , an affabi-
lity ioyned to a Grace, and
sweetnesse of behauiour,
which hath most power-
full charmes ouer soules,
naturally inclined to God-
nesse. It is nothing to do
well, if we do it not han-
somely : A benefit bestow-
ed with frownes is a
flinty

flinty loafe, not taken but out of necessity.

The third, an awakened, and wary prudence, well to discerne the dispositions, capacityes, manners, humors, affections, and pretentions of those with whom we converse, and to adapt our proceedings to the temper of euery one.

The fowrth ; Humility without sottishnesse, or seruile basenesse, ready to giue way to Reason, and not to presume of proper forces.

The fift, whereof we haue spoken heretofore, is, a discreete patience to

beare

beare with men, and oc-
cafions with out diftur-
bance, in fuch wife, that
you do euer keepe your
heart in a good ftate, yea
euen in vnexpected, and
difficult accidents. Who
well vnderftands this miftery, is worthy to com-
mand ouer men, vertue ha-
ueing allready placed him
in a degree neare vnto Angells. It is a good rule for
faire conuerfation to pro-
pofe to your felfe fome perfon noted to be of an exact
conuerfation, for your imitation, fo Saint Paule the
Apoftle faith to the Gala-
thians (according to the
Greeke Text) that he came

to

to historify the great Saint
Peter : For he beheld him
as an Historian should a
Monarch, whose prowesses
he is about to write, or as
a Painter should, a modell,
to draw out a Coppy.

So Saint Augustine sent
then to the conuersation of
Saint Paulinus, who desy-
red to profit in vertue: *Vade
in Campaniam, disce Paulinum.*
But the most effectuall precept is to thinke, how the
Word incarnate would con-
uerse were he in our place;
For then by his examples
we should do that, which
Ioseph did in Ægipt, of
whom the Scripture sayd
in the Psalme 104. (according

cording to the Hebrew)
that he hanged the Princes
of Phara's Court about his
heart.

The Reuerent Father
Gontery , a man of great
iudgment , and like vertue
hath written a litle Treatife
of conuerfation , wherein
he defcendeth fart into par-
ticulars. He who will read
it fhall in it find prudent
inftructions.

Conclufion of the Diurnall.

SECTION XII.

IN the euening before
Reft you are to make
Ff   Examen

Examen of Confcience,
which is the litle Confi-
ftory of the foule (as Philo
termeth it) where hauing
giuen thankes to God, and
inuoked his holy Grace,
you muft call your thoughtes, your wordes , your a-
ctions, your defects , and
neglects to an account,
That you may fee the
gaine, the loffe, and rec-
konings of that day , fo
to aduaunce good and cor-
rect euill , remitting the
one to difcretion , and
the other to the mercy of
God.

Remember that which
Saint Bernard fpake , (as
an oracle (in his booke
of

of the Interior house, That
one of the principall mir-
rors to behold God in, is,
*A reasonable soule which seeth
it selfe.* There, the Conscience must be set in a
Throne with a scepter in
hand, and all passions, and
imperfections at its feete.
There it should take the
liberty to say vnto you;
*Wicked seruant, behold a day
lost! What sluggishnesse at
your vprising! what negligence in your labour! what
wordes, and litle effect? To
what purpose is this curious in-
terrogation and temerarious iudgement; These wandring eyes,
these strayning thoughtes? Must*
Ff 2   *you*

you needs be offended for so small
a matter in such an occasion?
Must you so freely speake, and
murmur at the actions of ano-
ther? Must you take Repast so
sensually, and so greedily
seeke your ease in all kindes?
And so of the rest. But if
by the grace of God you
find some kind of vertues,
yet must you well examine,
& sift them, as the perfume
which was placed before
the Tabernacle, to present
them before the face of
God, and to say for con-
clusion with all humility,
what the holy man Father
Robert Southwell did. My
God I know what I haue
beene

beene (to wit) moſt wic-
ked; I know not what
I am, ſince I am ſtill vn-
certaine of the ſtate of grace.
I know not what I ſhall
be, being euery moment
doubtfull of my ſaluation.
God forgiue me what I
haue been, correct what
I am, direct what I ſhall
be. This done ſay the Li-
tanies, or ſome other vo-
call prayers, happily to
conclude the day with
Acts of Contrition, of
Faith, of Hope, of Pra-
yer for the liuing, and the
dead.

Say heere.

Light of immortall Spirits. Bright day which haſt no Euening ; Behold the world buryed in the darkneſſe of night, and this preſent day concluded, wherein I ſee (as in a Compendious Table) that my life ſhall haue an end. My God what benefits do I ſee on thy part, and what ingratitudes on mine ! Preſerue that in me, which is thine, and waſh away with the pretious bloud of thy Sonne, what is mine. Shelter me vnder the wings of thy protection

tection, among so many
shades, fantasies, and sna-
res of the father of darknesse, and graunt, though
mine eyes be closed vp in
sleepe, my heart may ne-
uer be shut against thy
loue.

Finally fall asleepe vpon
some good thought, that
(according to the Prophet)
your night may be illumi-
nated with the delights of
God: and if it happen you
be interrupted in your sleep,
supply it with iaculatory
prayers, and eleuations of
heart, as aunciently did the
Iust, called for this cause.
The Crickets of the night. By

this

this meanes you will lead a
life full of honour, repose,
and satisfaction within your
selfe, and you of euery day
shall make a stepp tow-
ards Eternity. The markes
which may, among others,
giue you a good hope of
your predestination, are
twelue principall.

1. A Faith liuely, simple,
and constant. 2. Purity of
life, which ordinarily is ex-
empt from grieuous sinnes.
3. Tribulation. 4. Clemency, and Mercy. 5. Pouerty
of spirit, disengaged from
the Earth. 6. Humility.
7. Charity towards your
neighbour. 8. Frequenta-
tion of the Sacraments of
Confession

Confeſſion and Commu-
nion. 9. Affection to the
word of God. 10. Reſi-
gnation of mind to the
will of your ſoueraigne
Maiſter. 11. Some notable
Act of Heroique vertue.
12. Deuotion towards our
bleſſed Lady in honour of
whom you ſhall do well
euery day to obſerue three
things. Firſt , to preſent
vnto her an oblation eue-
ry hower in the day of an
Aue , when at the ſtriking
of the clock you recall
your heart within it ſelfe.
Secondly, To practiſe ſome
mortification of ſpirit , or
body out of a motiue of the
imitation

imitation of her vertues.
Thirdly, To giue some Al-
mes eyther spirituall, or
temporall in her honour.

You will find this Diur-
nall litle in bulke, and great
in efficacy, if to rellish it
well, you begin to practise
it. It containeth many
things, which deserue to
be meditated at leysure:
For they are serious and
sage precepts selected from
the choyce of the morall
doctrine of holy Fathers:
But if they seeme short,
they are not there fore to
be the lesse valued : Re-
member the braue wor-
keman Myrmecides em-
ployed

ployed more time to make
a Bee, then a silly Architect did to build a House.

THE END.

Prayse be to God.

A DAILY

A DAILY EXCERCISE,
when you rise.

Benedicta sit sancta, & indiuidua Trinitas, nunc & semper & per infinita seçula seçulorum, Amen. Pater, Aue, Credo, Confiteor, &c.

Prayer.

Domine Deus omnipotens qui ad principium huius diei nos peruenire fecisti, tua nos hodie salua virtute, vt in hac die ad nullum declinemus peccatum, sed semper ad tuam iustitiam faciendam nostra proce-

cedant eloquia, dirigantur
cogationes, & opera. Per
Christum Dominum no-
strum. Amen.

To your Angell-Guardian.

ANgele Dei qui custos
es mei me tibi commis-
sum pietate superna serua,
defende, guberna. Amen.

In the beginning of Actions.

ACtiones nostras quęsu-
mus Domine, aspiran-
do præueni, & adiuuando
prosequere, vt cuncta nostra
oratio, & operatio à te
semper incipiat & per te cæ-
pta finiatur. Per Christum
Dominum nostrum. Amen.

In the end of our Actions.

SVſcipe , clementiſſime
Deus precibus & meritis
beatæ Mariæ ſemper Virgi-
nis, & omnium Sanctorum,
& Sanctarum, officium ſer-
uitutis : & ſi quid laude egi-
mus propitius reſpice , &
quod negligenter actum eſt,
clementer ignoſce. Qui in
Trinitate perfecta viuis &
regnas , Deus, per omnia
ſçcula ſeculorum. Amen.

In the Euening.

TE lucis ante terminum,
Rerum Creator poſci-
Vt ſolita clementia, (mus,
Sis prçſul ad cuſtodiam.

Procul

Procul recedant somnia,
Et noctium phantasmata,
Hostemque nostrum com-
    prime,
Ne polluantur corpora.

  Præsta Pater omnipotens,
Per Iesum Christum Domi-
    num,
Qui tecum in perpetuum,
Regnat cum sancto Spiritu.
Amen.

  Salua nos, Domine vi-
gilantes, custodi nos dor-
mientes : vt vigilemus cum
Christo, & requiescamus in
pace. Custodi nos domine
vt pupillam oculi : Sub vm-
bra alarum tuarum protege
nos. Dignare Domine nocte
ista, sine peccato nos custo-
dire. Miserere nostri Domi-
       ne,

ne, Miserere nostri : Fiat
misericordia tua super nos,
quemadmodum sperauimus
in te. Domine exaudi ora-
tionem meam , & clamor
meus ad te veniat.

A Prayer.

VIsita quæsumus Domine
habitationem istam , &
omnes insidias inimici ab ea
longè repelle : Angeli tui
sancti habitent in ea, qui
nos in pace custodiant, &
benedictio tua sit super nos
semper. Per Christum Do-
minum nostrum. Amen.

Denont

DEVOVT
ASPIRATIONS
FOR THE ACTIONS,
of the Day.

In the Morning.

Will pray vnto thee in
the morning : In the
morning thou wilt heare
my prayer. *Pfal. 5.*

Thou shalt enlighten me
with the rayes of thy face,
and the wild beastes of the
forrest (which are Paſſiõs)
shall returne into their den-
nes. *Pfal. 103.*

My dayes are as the dayes
Gg of

of a Hireling, vntill the day
of Eternity rife ouer me, &
that the shadowes of the
night of this world, are dif-
pelled. *Iob.* 7 and *Cant.* 4.

*At the beginning of a
good worke.*

It is written of me in the
beginning of thy booke;
that I do thy commaund-
ments; my God I will, for I
beare thy law engrauen in
the midft of my heart. *Pſ.* 39

In good Inſpirations.

God hath opened the ea-
res of my heart, and I will
beware how I gain-ſay him.
Iſay 50.

For Maſſe.

I will go, and I will ſee
this

this great vision. *Exod. 3.*

O how louely are thy Ta-
bernacles. , Lord God of
Hoaftes. *Pfal. 6 3.*

At fpirituall leſſon.
Speake o Lord for thy
feruāt hearkneth. *1. Kings 3.*

When you ſpeake.

My heart hath vttered a
good word, and I will tell
my workes to the King.
Pfal. 44.

At refeɛtion:
Thou openeſt thy hand,
and filleſt euery creature
with thy bleſſing. *Pſal.144.*

In proſperity.
Let my tongue cleaue to
my palate, if I remember not
thee in the beginning of all

my ioy , and prosperities.
Psal. 136.

In *Aduersity.*

God mortyfieth, and quickeneth. I. *Kings* .2.

If we haue receyued good from the hands of God, why should we not receyue ill? *Iob.* 2.

Ought not Christ to haue suffered these things, and so to enter into his glory? *Luc.* 24.

In the *affaires, and cares of the world.*

Man passeth as a shadow, and he is troubled in vaine. *Psal.* 38.

In *Calumnyes.*

If I did please men, I should not be the seruant

of

of God. *Galat.* 1.

In prayſes.

Not to vs, O Lord, not
to vs but to thee be glory
giuen. *Pſal.* 113.

*Againſt the vaine hopes of
the world.*

Lord in thy holy Citty
thou ſhalt reduce all the
vaine imaginations of men
to nothing, as the dreame
of a night. *Pſal.* 72.

Againſt Pride.

He that exalteth himſelfe
ſhall be humbled. *Luc.* 14.

Againſt Couetouſneſſe.

It is a more bleſſed thing
to giue, thē to take: *Aſt.* 20

Againſt

Againſt Luſt.

Know you not that your bodies are the members of Chriſt? *Cor. c. 6. 10. 15.*

Againſt Enuy.

He who loueth not his neighbour , dwelleth in death. *1. Iohn. 3.*

Againſt Gloutony.

The Kingdome of heauen, is neither meate, nor drincke. *Rom. 14.*

Againſt Anger.

Learne of me, for I am humble & meeke of heart: *Math. 11.*

Againſt Sloth.

Curſed be he who doth the worke of God negligently. *Hier. 48.*

Rules

Rules of Faith.

Passe not the limits which thy Fore-fathers haue sett thee: Prouerb. 12.

There is no other author of the Knowledge of God, but God himself, and necessarily we must learne of God what we are to belieue of God. *S. Hilary* 1. *of the Trinity.*

God calleth vs not to Beatitude by difficult questions. It is enough we seeke for him with simplicity of heart to make profession of his seruice with sincere piety. *Idem.*

Many weight considerations very iustly hold me in the bosome of the Catholique Church; The consent of people, and nations: The authority of the Church it selfe ; which is risen from miracles , is nourished by Hope, encreased by charity, and established by its antiquity : The succession of Bishopps , holdes me in it, which beginning by the Sea, and authority of S. Peter (vnto whom God recommended the care of his flock) hath mainteyned it selfe to this present. Lastly the name of Catholique holds me in it. *S. August. in his booke de vtilitate credendi*

dendi, & contra epist. Fudam.

It is an extreme folly to dispute against belieffes, generally receyued into the Church. *S. August. Epist.* 18.

Let vs follow generality, antiquity, consent : Let vs hold what was held, throughout euery where, & by all, so that it be authorized by the diuine law, and by the Traditions of the Catholique Church.

Not to know any thing beyond it, is to know all. *Vincent Lyrin.* A*gainst profane Noueltyes. Tertulian in his prescriptions.*

An Act of Faith.

O Lord I belieue. ayd my in-

incredulity. *Mar.* 9.

I know my Redeemer liueth. *Iob.* 9.

An Act of Hope.

Allthough I should walke in the midst of the shadowes of death, I will not feare euill, becaufe (O my God) thou art with me. *Pfal.* 12.

With him I am in Tribulation, and I will glorify him. *Pfal.* 90.

An Act of Charity.

What haue I to defire in heauen, and what haue I to aske of thee on earth ? my flefh and my heart fainteth,

O

O the God of my heart, &
my portion for all eternity.
Pſal. 72.

O my Soueraigne Paſtor
feed me thy poore ſupply-
ant with the ceaſeleſſe influ-
ence of thy Diuinity. This
I begg, this I deſire with all
my heart, that thy feruent
loue may penetrate me into
the bottome of my ſoule, &
transforme me wholy into
thee. *Bloſius.*

PRAYER

PRAYER FOR EVERY DAY of the Weeke.

FOR SVNDAY.

To the blessed Trinity.

1. TV Trinitatis vnitas,
Orbem potenter qui
regis,
Attende laudum cantica,
Quę excubantes psallimus.

Te manè laudum carmine,
Te deprecemur vesperè.
Te nostra supplex gloria,
Per cuncta laudet sęcula.

Tibi laus, tibi gloria, tibi
gratiarum actio in sęcula
sempi-

sempiterna, et benedictum
nomen gloriæ tuæ sanctum,
et laudabile, & superexalta-
tum in sæcula, ô beata Trinitas.

Verf. Benedicamus patrem,
et filium, cum sancto spiritu.
Resp. Laudemus, et super
exaltemus eum in sæcula.

Oremus.

OMnipotens sempiterne
Deus, qui dedisti famu-
lis tuis, in confessione veræ
fidei, æternæ Trinitatis glo-
riam agnoscere, & in poten-
tia maiestatis adorare vnita-
tem : quæsumus & eiusdem
fidei firmitate ab omnibus
semper muniamur aduersis.
Per Dominum.

FOR

FOR MONDAY.

To the holy Ghost.

2. VEni creator Spiritus,
   Métes tuorum visita:
Imple superna gratia,
Quæ tu creasti pectora.

  Qui paracletus diceris,
Donum Dei altissimi:
Fons viuus, ignis, charitas,
Et spiritalis vnctio.

   Tu septiformis munere,
Dextrę Dei tu digitus:
Tu rite promissum Patris,
Sermone ditans guttura.

   Accęnde lumen sensibus,
Infunde amorem cordibus,
Infirma nostri corporis
Virtute firmans perpeti.

                     Hostem

Hoſtem repellas longius,
Pacemque dones protinus:
Ductore ſic te præuio,
Vitemus omne noxium.

Per te ſciamus da Patrem,
Noſcamus atque Filium,
Te vtriuſque Spiritum,
Credamus omni tempore.

Gloria Patri Domino,
Natóque qui à mortuis
Surrexit, atque Paracleto,
In ſæculorum ſæcula. Amen.

A prayer.

DEvs qui corda fidelium
ſancti Spiritus illuſtra-
tione docuiſti : da nobis in
eodem ſpiritu recta ſapere,
& de eius ſemper conſola-
tione gaudere. Per Domi-
num noſtrum, &c. In vni-
tate eiuſdem Spiritus ſancti.

FOR

FOR TVESDAY.

To the holy name of Iesus.

3. IEsu nostra redemptio
Amor & desiderium:
Deus creator omnium,
Homo in fine temporum;

Quæ te vicit clementia
Vt ferres nostra crimina,
Crudelem mortem patiens
Vt nos à morte tolleres!

Inferni claustra penetrans
Tuos captiuos redimens,
Victor triumpho nobili,
Ad dextram Patris residens.

Ipsa te cogat pietas,
Vt mala nostra superes
Parcendo, & voti compotes
Nos tuo vultu saties.

Tu

Tu esto nostrum gaudium
Qui es futurus præmiûm,
Sit nostra in te gloria,
Per cuncta semper sęcula.
Amen.

Prayer.

DOmine Iesu Christe,
qui dixisti, petite, &
accipietis, quærite & in-
uenietis. pulsate & ope-
rietur vobis ; quæsumus
da nobis petentibus diui-
nissimi tui amoris affectum,
vt te toto corde, & opere
diligamus, & à tua nun-
quam laude cessemus.

Hh

FOR

FOR WEDNESDAY.

To the Angells.

4. CVstodes hominum
psallimus Angelos
Naturæ fragili, quos pater
addidit
Cœlestis comites, insidian-
tibus,
Ne succumberet hostibus.
Nam quos corrueret pro-
ditor Angelus
Concessis meritò pulsus ho-
noribus,
Ardens inuidia, pellere ni-
titur,
Quos cælo Deus aduocat.
Huc custos igitur peruigil
aduola

aduola,   (dita,
Auertens patria de tibi cre-
Tam morbos animi quam
   requiescere
Quicquid non finit incolas.
   Sanctæ sit Triadi laus pia
   iugiter
Cuius perpetuo numine
   machina
Triplex hæc regitur, cuius
   in omnia
Regnat gloria sæcula.

Prayer.

DEus, qui ineffabili pro-
uidentia sanctos Ange-
los tuos ad nostram custo-
diam mittere dignaris largi-
re supplicibus tuis, & eorum
semper protectione defen-
di, & æterna societate gau-
       H h 2   dere

dere. Per dominum nostrum
Iesum Christum , filium
tuum, qui tecum viuit & regnat, &c.

FOR THVRSDAY.

To the blessed Sacrament.

5. PAnge lingua gloriosi
   Corporis mysterium,
Sanguinisque pretiosi,
Quem in mundi pretium
Fructus ventris generosi
R ex effudit gentium.

  Nobis datus , nobis natus
Ex intacta virgine
Et in mundo conuersatus
Sparso verbi semine ,
Sui moras incolatus
Miro clausit ordine.

                        In

In supremę noᶜte cęnæ
Recumbens cum fratribus:
Obseruata lege plenè
Cibis in legalibus
Cibum turbę duodenæ
Se dat suis manibus.

Verbum Caro panem ve-
Verbum carnem efficit: (rū,
Fitque , sanguis Christi me-
Et si sensus deficit :   (rum,
Ad firmandum cor sincerum
Sola fides sufficit.

Tantum ergo Sacramentū
Veneremur cernui :
Et antiquum documentum
Nouo cedat ritui:
Præstet fides supplemētum,
Sensuum defeᶜtui.

Genitori, Genitoque
Laus, & iubilatio,
Salus, honor virtus quoque
                              Sit

Sit & benedictio:
Procedenti, ab vtroque
Compar sit laudatio. Amen,

Prayer.

DEus, qui nobis sub Sacramento mirabili passionis tuę memoriam reliquisti tribue quæsumus, ita nos corporis, & saguinis tui sacra mysteria venerari, vt redemptionis tuæ fructum in nobis iugiter sentiamus. Qui viuis & regnas in vnitate spiritus sancti Deus per omnia sęcula sæculorum. Amen.

FOR FRIDAY.

Of the Passion.

Domine

Domine Iesu Christe, a-
doro te in Cruce pen-
dentem, coronam spineam
in capite portantem, deprecor te, vt me tua Crux libe-
ret ab Angelo percutiente.

Pater noster. Aue Maria.

O Domine Iesu Christe,
adoro te in cruce vul-
neratum, felle & aceto po-
tatum: deprecor te, vt vulne-
ra tua sint remedium ani-
mę meę. Amen.

Pater noster. Aue Maria.

O Domine Iesu Christe,
propter illam amari-
tudinem, quam pro me mi-
serrimo

ſerrimo ſuſtinuiſti in cruce,
maximè in illa hora quando
nobiliſſima anima tua egreſ-
ſa eſt de benedicto corpore
tuo : deprecor te miſerere a-
nimæ meæ in egreſſu ſuo, &
perduc eam in vitam æter-
nam. Amen.

Pater noſter. Aue Maria.

O Domine Ieſu Chriſte,
adoro te in ſepulchro
poſitum, Myrrha & aroma-
tibus conditum : deprecor
te, vt tua mors ſis vita mea.
Amen.

Pater noſter. Aue Maria.

O Domine Ieſu Chriſte,
adoro te deſcenden-
tem

tem ad inferos, & liberantem captiuos: deprecor te, ne permittas me illuc introire, Amen.

Pater noster. Aue Maria.

O Domine Iesu Christe adoro te resurgentem à mortuis, ascendentem ad cęlos sedentemque ad dextram Patris: Deprecor te vt illuc te sequi, & tibi præsentari merear. Amen.

Pater noster. Aue Maria.

O Domine Iesu Christe Pastor bonę, iustos cōserua, peccatores iustifica, omnibus fidelibus miserere,

&

& propitius esto mihi pec-
catori. Amen.

Pater noster. Aue Maria.

FOR SATVRDAY.

*To the Conception of our blessed
Lady.*

SAlua mundi domina
Cælorum regina:
Salue Virgo virginum,
Stella Matutina
Salue plena Gratię,
Clara lux diuina:
Mundi in auxilium
Domina festina.
Ab æterno Dominus,
Te preordinauit
Matrem

Vnige-

Vnigeniti
Verbi, quo creauit
Terram, pontum, ęthera:
Te pulchram ornauit
Sibi ſponſam, in qua
Adam non peccauit.

Verſ. Elegit eam Deus, &
preelegit eam.

Reſp. In tabernaculo ſuo ha-
bitare fecit eam.

Verſ. Domine exaudi ora-
tionem meam.

Reſp. Et clamor meus ad te
veniat.

Prayer.

SAncta Maria, Regina cę-
lorum, mater Domini
noſtri Ieſu Chriſti & mundi
Domina, quę nullum dere-
linquis, & nullum deſpicis,
reſpice me Domina clemen-
ter

ter, oculo pietatis, & impetra
mihi apud tuum dilectum
Filium cunctorum veniam
peccatorum : vt qui nunc
tuam sanctam Conceptio-
nem deuoto affectu recolo,
æternę in futurum beatitu-
dinis brauium capiam, ipso
quem virgo peperisti do-
nante Domino nostro Iesu
Christo, qui cum Patre &
sancto spiritu viuit & regnat
in Trinitate perfecta, Deus
in sęcula sęculorum. Amen.

It will do well to say seauen times, at seauen sundry
howers of the day, these
prayers according to your
deuotion, and conueniency.

THE END.

Faultes escaped.

IN the Profession of Faith
art. 14. line 2. *read* be;
page 19. lin. 18. and 19. *read*
thee. pag. 74. l. 4. *read* your.
p. 84. l. laſt, *read* is. pag. 211
l. 1. *read* to. pag. 120. l. laſt,
read the. pag. 326. lin. 14.
read he.